Aunt Barb's

Bread Book

BY

Barbara Swell

ISBN 9781883206628   Order No. NGB834
Library of Congress Control Number:
2011930953
©2011 by Native Ground Music, Inc.
Asheville, North Carolina
International Copyright Secured.
All rights reserved.

A.M. WICKSON

FETCH YOUR DOUGHBOWL

Nobody would trade sandwiches with me in the 1963 lunchroom of John Street Elementary School in Martinsburg, West Virginia. And I mean NOBODY. While the other kids passed soft white sandwich halves and factory-made spongy pink cupcakes back and forth, there I sat with my brown speckled whole wheat sandwich and apple. I coveted my friends' fluffy white bread sandwiches with the crusts removed and the grape jelly oozing out through the soggy middles. I even had a friend who used to sit on his lunchbag all morning so that his balloon bread and jelly sandwich would be perfectly flat and purple come lunchtime. I don't think my mother ever once brought squishy white bread into the house. And, wouldn't you know, neither have I.

The white vs. whole-grain bread battle has been going on for a long time. Centuries. Believe me, there's nothing new when it comes to so-called health breads vs. white flour breads. Well, maybe there's one thing new these days ... it used to be that the wealthier you were, the more refined your flour. Now it appears to be the other way around; the better your grain and the more it maintains its integrity at the skilled hands of both the miller and the baker, the more expensive the bread.

Though whole grain breakfast "gems" were invited to the tables of most Americans by the mid-1800s, it's the ungentrified, coarse family breads of the regular people who didn't have servants, cooks and nannies that I love most. Recipes for regional breads which were the daily fare of settlers, farm families, and small town dwellers rarely made it into cookbooks before the Civil War. Every country housekeeper baked her family bread weekly from whatever flours were available and specific methods occasionally showed up in farm magazines, handwritten recipe journals, or folksy literary works. It's from these early to mid-19th century sources that I've learned to make most of the tasty, wholesome breads that you'll find in this book.

LET'S MAKE BREAD!

American bread preferences changed dramatically in the 1870s as modern roller-mills made refined wheats and other grains more accessible and affordable. By 1907, professional bakers were exasperated by the public demand for puffy white, quick-rise tasteless breads like those composed by housewives following their explicit, modern domestic science cookery books. Whole grains did, however, reappear briefly, during both world wars and then again in the back-to-the-land era of the 1960s and 70s.

Today's artisan bread movement is gaining popularity as flavorful, regionally adapted heritage grains find their way back into the dough bowls of more and more American bakers. If you want to make great old-timey breads, let the grains that are available in your area take center stage in your breads. You'll have to experiment with your recipes, but that's fun! Even bad homemade bread is edible.

Speaking of bad bread, I've made plenty of it while writing this book. You'd think that after several decades of baking bread I'd be pretty good at it. All I can say is that until you try and raise a loaf of bread from temperamental seething ale barm, hops-yeast and potato starters, you haven't lived. And if, when you read this book, you find the recipes too vague, here's what I had to work with:

Cook Book, Debbie Coleman, 1855 *"Put the bread in sponge with milk, warm water, sour milk, or milk and water. When very light, make it into soft dough and let it rise in a dough-trough. Then put it into pans and let it rise a second time. When light, bake."*

It would break my heart to convert such prose into exact measurements. Still, the story behind this recipe and so many more like it, is one worth sharing. So, the first half of this book tells the tale of yesterday's American breads and the particulars of how to re-create these great loaves using old-time methods. The second half of the book contains the recipes.

Enjoy your baking!

LOVE AND DOUGH

NANCY. AN IDYL OF THE KITCHEN
The Century Illustrated Magazine, Dec. 1883

In brown Holland apron she stood in the kitchen;
Her sleeves were rolled up, and her cheeks all aglow;
Her hair was coiled neatly; when I, indiscreetly,
Stood watching while Nancy was kneading the dough.

Now, who could be neater, or brighter, or sweeter,
Or who hum a song so delightfully low,
Or who look so slender, so graceful, so tender,
As Nancy, sweet Nancy, while kneading the dough?

How deftly she pressed it, and squeezed it, caressed it,
And twisted and turned it, now quick and now slow.
Ah, me, but that madness I've paid for in sadness!
'Twas my heart she was kneading as well as the dough.

At last, when she turned for her pan to the dresser,
She saw me and blushed, and said shyly, " Please, go"
Or my bread I'll be spoiling, in spite of my toiling,
If you stand here and watch while I'm kneading the dough."

I begged for permission to stay. She'd not listen;
The sweet little tyrant said, "No, sir! no! no!"
Yet when I had vanished on being thus banished,
My heart staid with Nancy while kneading the dough.

I'm dreaming, sweet Nancy, and see you in fancy;
Your heart, love, has softened and pitied my woe,
And we, dear, are rich in a dainty wee kitchen
Where Nancy, my Nancy, stands kneading
the dough.

~John A. Fraser, Jr.

CONTENTS

How to Use This Book

All the historic recipes in this book are recorded as found. You'll find them dated and in italics. They're great fun to play with, but don't get your knickers in a twist if your bread doesn't turn out as you hoped the first time around. Under selected historic recipes, I've included an updated version that should produce a good bread. Keep in mind, though, it takes practice to produce a decent loaf of bread from any era. It's helpful to jot down any recipe adjustments you make in your dough-splattered cookbook.

Our recipe testers were quite surprised by the amount of tending these breads took. But if we look back to bread baking day in the mid to late 1900s, housewives were every bit as busy as you are today. It's just that they took a whole day out of their week to do the family baking, and in between minding their dough, they were feeding chickens, managing the cookstove, diapering the baby and running the homestead. The big difference is that they were around. And you might not want to be. Learning about retarding your dough in the refrigerator will go a long way to helping you fit your bread into your own busy schedule. (See page 27.) For now, here are some things to keep in mind as you get out your bread bowl:

These delicious breads are not quick and easy. At least not until you get used to making them. They are all made with an overnight "sponge" which is a pre-ferment that adds loads of flavor and texture to your bread. But, it's one more thing to remember. A mature, risen sponge will keep in your fridge for three days until you get around to baking and you don't need to warm it up when you're ready to use it. You can omit the sponge from these recipes as long as you add the sponge ingredients to the dough recipe and double the yeast.

No special equipment is needed in order to reproduce the breads in this book other than what's already in your kitchen. The various recommended pots and pans mentioned are optional. A loaf pan will bake all these breads just fine.

How to Use This Book

Most American bakers (and bread book authors) now include metric weights for recipe ingredients. Our grandmothers used the gill, teacup, quart, ounce and pound measurements. However, I find that flour is the only ingredient that varies wildly at the hands of the baker enough to ruin your loaf. So I'm offering flour in metric weights as well as in cups. Based on my experience as a cooking instructor, for this book one cup flour = 130 grams. (See resources, page 67 for scales.)

A digital instant-read thermometer is helpful.. A 65° dough takes much longer to rise than one at 76°. Unless your dough is taking a spell in your fridge to slow its fermentation, 76° is dandy. Internal temperature also informs you of when your bread is baked.

Use fine salt, not Kosher. All purpose (AP) and bread flours yield different results. You'll have better bread if you use the suggested flours. Flaked kosher salts weigh less than fine salt. Fine sea salt that's not iodized is best for breads.

For those who are new to bread-craft, I highly recommend that you get yourself a comprehensive, instructive, illustrated bread baking book. (See recommended reading, page 68.) But if you really want to learn to bake good bread, find somebody to teach you in person. So much of baking is tactile and you just can't tell the desired hydration, texture, or aroma from reading a book or even watching a video.

Oh, and did I mention the part about practice? For better or worse, your breads will teach you something every time you bake!

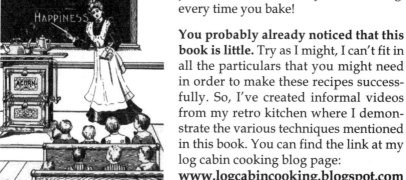

You probably already noticed that this book is little. Try as I might, I can't fit in all the particulars that you might need in order to make these recipes successfully. So, I've created informal videos from my retro kitchen where I demonstrate the various techniques mentioned in this book. You can find the link at my log cabin cooking blog page:
www.logcabincooking.blogspot.com

FINE HOMEMADE BREAD

Before we go even one step further, let's have a chat about what kinds of breads you like. People can be downright pig-headed when it comes to what they believe is a fine loaf of bread. Take my husband, Wayne, for example. He has discovered what he thinks is the perfect bread made by the best baker ever, who just happens to be our friend, David, of Farm & Sparrow bakery in Asheville. Indeed, I cannot imagine that a wood-fired oven baked artisan bread can get any better. Crafted from heritage grains he grows in partnership with a local farmer, David's home-milled, open-crumbed breads are naturally

David and Wayne

fermented, lovingly tended, baked in a grand oven and are a sight to behold. And to eat!

On the other hand, you might long for the silky-soft, flour-dusted, cream-colored buttermilk potato rolls your grandmother

Farm & Sparrow Hearth-Baked Loaves

used to make. And, who among you got your start with the back-to-the-land 1970s sturdy, whole grain, homesteader loaves that you baked in your rural farmhouse cookstove? (That would be me. Thankfully, my loaves are not so sturdy now!)

There's something for just about everybody in this little book. Bear in mind, though, that our American great-grandmothers had a palate for fine-crumbed, soft-crusted breads with no hint of sour flavor. See facing page for testimonials. And certainly, you'll find the quantity of salt in historic breads quite low by today's standards. I've included updated versions of most of the vintage recipes in this book, but please feel free to adjust ingredients up or down to suit your own tastes. If you're interested in crusty, holey artisan breads, have a look at the wild yeast and the un-kneaded breads, and see page 68 for additional reading.

FINE HOMEMADE BREAD

EVIL HARD BREAD - "In baking bread, it is desirable to avoid the evils of hardness on the one hand and pastiness on the other; nor should it be sour, dense or heavy. It should have thorough and uniform kneading, so that the carbonic acid will not be liberated in excess in any one place, forming hollows, or "eyes," and detaching the crumb from the crust. The vesicles should be numerous, small and equally disseminated, nor should the crust be bitter and black, but of an aromatic agreeable flavor. The color of the crumb, unless in the case of whole wheaten bread, should be white, and should be free from acidity or sourness. It should keep sweet and eatable for several days"

~Complete Bread Baker, J. Thompson Gill 1881

"The dread of all bakers is sour bread."
~Atwater, 1900

HORNY BREAD - "Some one house-keeper may gain a reputation for her superlative bread which has become a subject of pride to all her friends, but on examination what do we find? A bread excellently white and light, perhaps having pores as coarse as honey-comb, with a very thin crust which flakes like a soda cracker, yet on the second day this bread becomes horny and quite lacking in flavor. Such bread is made from a thick batter without kneading.

Another housekeeper prides herself upon the exceeding fine grain of her bread and is horror-stricken if a hole the size of a pea appears. Many women consider this fine texture the essential point to aim at. Probably the best bread is between these two extremes."

~American Kitchen Magazine, 1900

HEARTH-BAKED BREADS

I n his curious 1837 book, called *A Treatise on Bread*, Sylvester Graham instructs us that "While the dough is rising, preparations should be made for baking it. Some bake their bread in a brick oven, some in a stove, some in a reflector, and some in a baking kettle. Good bread-makers, accustomed to brick ovens, can always manage them with a very great degree of certainty; and as a general fact, bread is sweeter, baked in this way, than in any other.

Yet, when it is well baked in tin reflectors, it is certainly very fine; and so it is also when well baked in iron stoves."

DR. CHAUNCEY'S PATENT
AIR TIGHT

COOKING STOVES.

Tin reflector ovens such as this one were placed before an open hearth and the radiant heat from the fire did a darn good job of baking the bread that lay on the shelves.

But what if you don't have a wood-fired brick bread oven and you want to produce a well-baked loaf of wholesome bread? Don't fret. Sometimes, the less you have to work with, the more creative and effective are the ideas you come up with.

You can bake in cast iron pans or Dutch ovens, under an earthenware cloche, or on a granite or ceramic stone placed in your range. Nothing bakes bread like a footed iron pot nestled in fireplace embers. But if your heart's set on an outside bread oven, it needn't be fancy. Adobe, cinderblock, makeshift tin ovens ... even a Weber grill fitted with round baking stone and vented through the top, all do the job and make bread baking an adventure.

RADIANT HEAT BAKING

Wjhen our earliest European-American ancestors weren't baking their breads on the hearth floor or on heated hoes or wooden boards set near the fire, they used an assortment of iron pots to produce their "staff of life." Breads were dropped into cast iron bake kettles with feet and rimmed tops and then placed on live coals and covered with embers at the fire's edge to bake. If you were of "gentle birth," your individual rolls might have been baked in a bread oven built into the side of the kitchen hearth. Those less fortunate made do with kettle breads made at home or loaves produced by the village baker.

By the end of the 19th century, most American homes were equipped with iron or metal cookstoves that were fired by wood, coal, or gas. Hearths in newer homes were built for warmth rather than cooking. Housewives still baked their whole grain gem muffins in cast iron pans, but graniteware metal pans were now the preferred vehicle for bread baking.

By the early 20th century, homemade radiant heat-baked breads were becoming but a dim memory in many parts of the country when, lo and behold, along comes the 1920s motor-picnicking movement. Cast iron cooking pots were dusted off and packed onto the floorboards of Model-T's, and homemade breads were once again plopped into campfire-heated Dutch ovens to bake. Iron pot baked breads have since been relegated to the world of camping and homesteading until a few years ago when Dutch oven baked, artisan-style breads once again made a welcome comeback. And that brings us to now. Let's go iron pot shopping!

> Iron is not a good conductor of heat, but once it's hot, it stays hot. If you're baking with a cast iron Dutch oven with live coals at the fire's edge, you'll need to rotate it periodically in order to keep the heat even.

CAST IRON PANS

IRON POT SHOPPING

Antique cast iron cookware is generally my first choice not only for the workmanship, but also because of the vast variety of shapes and sizes that were made in the past. Much of the vintage iron cookware available today was manufactured in the mid-19th century and can be had for affordable prices at yard sales, online stores and antique shops. When buying antique ironware, I look for pans that have been in use or whose history is attainable. Some people coat pans with paint or blacking products to cover flaws for display. I'd give these pans a miss. (See page 70 for care and cleaning tips.)

I highly recommend using American-made cast ironware because it's reliably well-made. Lodge is the only operating American manufacturer of iron cookware and their wide assortment of quality products now come pre-seasoned and ready to use. French-made enameled cast ironware is wonderful as well. Keep in mind that a well-made iron pot, be it young or old, is forever.

Iron pots can be heavy, so you want the smallest size that does the job. I have a 5-qt. antique Dutch oven I found at a yard sale for $25, and it can be seen in photos throughout the book. My pot works great but it could be a bit heavy for some. You can bake in enameled iron pots, just unscrew and remove the knob and stuff the screw hole with foil.

To make the recipes in this book, it's helpful to have one or more of these pans: (For sources, see page 66.)
- 3, 4 or 5-quart Dutch oven with lid, flat bottomed
- Footed, camp Dutch oven with recessed lid
- Iron gem pan, antique or new (Lodge's drop biscuit pan)
- Ceramic "cloche" with bell top also makes great bread
- Bakestone, either ceramic or granite if baking "potless"

DON'T bake any of these breads in nonstick muffin or bread pans because most are not suited for high-heat baking.

GRAINS

No discussion of bread making would be complete without paying homage to our ancient ancestors who domesticated and, at times, gave their lives for access to the grains we now often take for granted in our daily hunk of American bread. Speaking of which, what I love about American bread is that there is no American bread. Our loaves are a fusion of the many food traditions of those who have settled in this country starting with the native people who were here long before European explorers ever arrived.

Vintage cookbooks are chock full of ethnic and regional breads made from a variety of wheats, corn, rye, barley, buckwheat, oats and rice. But nothing beats the breads born of a grain shortage. Nineteenth century Americans benefitted from the French ingenuity of substituting apples, turnips, potatoes, squash and even beans for scarce wheat in their breads. World War I brought with it the unfortunate opportunity for American bakers to wander away from their reliance on hard spring wheats and return to using a variety of grains for family bread. But, for the most part, we now count on wheat for the bulk of our breads, so here's a brief primer on the sorts you might find in your bag of flour.

Hard red spring wheat varieties are grown in harsh northern climates like Minnesota, Montana, and the Dakotas. They're planted in the spring and harvested in the summer. Hard red spring wheat has a high protein content (12-14%) and is what ends up as bread flour.

Hard red winter wheats are grown mostly in Kansas, Nebraska, Oklahoma and Texas. They are planted in the fall and harvested in the summer, have a medium amount of protein (9-12%), and are good for bread. Especially the breads in this book that contain an overnight sponge.

Hard white wheat is OK for bread; it's milder tasting than the red wheats.

Soft white and red wheats are low in protein (8-10%) and not suitable for breads, but they make a dandy biscuit, gem and piecrust.

Durum wheat (semolina) is grown in North Dakota and is the hardest of wheats, used mostly in pasta and sometimes as an addition to bread.

THE MILLER

Much mystique surrounds the early American miller. Was he the folk hero with the beautiful winsome daughter skillfully grinding his neighbor's wheat, or the villain suspected of sneaking adulterants and extra bran into his customer's entire wheat flour? Well, maybe both. Whichever the case, the high extraction, bran and germ flecked grist mill flours were surely missed by many bakers once large mechanized roller mills came into production in the 1870s.

Where finely bolted white flour rolls were once the staff-of-life of the genteel class, now machine-sifted, snowy loaves were available for all at affordable prices. By 1889, an insurrection led by home cooks and physicians alike was rising with rants like these:

"Our American fondness for fine white bread is a serious injury to our health, as we bolt and rebolt our flour until we extract from it three-quarters of its nutritive qualities. American Farm and Home Magazine, 1889

"Really good corn meal is hard to obtain nowadays. The modern roller processes of crushing grains have banished much of the flavor as well as the healthfulness of all meals and flours. The flouring-mill proprietors are discussing the introduction of stones to supply a demand for ground wheat flour that seems to be springing up, and if this is done we may have a better chance to obtain good corn meal also." Good Housekeeping, September, 1889

By happy chance for you, though, today's America has a bounty of historic grist mills that you can visit and many have locally grown and ground flours and meals available for purchase. Pop your flour and cornmeal into the freezer as soon as possible to preserve the flavor. And if you really want fresh flours, be your own miller. I often mill my flours with a hand-mill which helps me to work off the bread carbs, but electric mills will do as well. (See resources, page 67, for regional and home mill sources.)

FLOUR

The completion of the transcontinental railroad in 1869, linking cities in the Far West with those in the East, brought big changes to America's bread bowls. Large, modern mills in the upper Midwest were now able to ship their flours throughout the country, signaling a threat to regionally grown and neighborhood-milled flours. Before the 1870s, most Americans made their breads from whatever grains grew closest to home. The characteristics of available flours gave way to beloved traditional breads, rolls and biscuits. Some of these breads live on, some have been lost, like southern rice and hominy gems.

Even so, good things have come of national flour availability. From my vintage cabin in the mountains of Western North Carolina, where lower protein flours are the norm, I happily load my chewy bialys made from hard spring wheats grown in Montana into our old wood cookstove. But my everyday naturally fermented breads are mostly made from Carolina-grown wheats, and I, likewise, have learned to adapt my breads to available flours.

If you're new to bread making, it's best to start with good flours that behave predictably due to careful treatment at the mill. All the recipes in this book were tested with King Arthur flours which should be available in most grocery stores nationwide. Once you gain experience, I encourage you to also bake with the sustainably-farmed grains grown and milled closest to where you live. The whole grains I used to bake these breads include North and South Carolina heritage varieties of rye, wheat, and corn, milled close to my home in Asheville, N. C. Your own local grains will, no doubt, bring their own unique charms to your loaves.

Breads made with long fermentation times like the ones herein, benefit from all-purpose (AP) flours with a protein content of 10-12%. King Arthur AP flour is 11.7% and is just right for any of these recipes. Other national brands may be fine as well, just give them a try, and adjust recipes as needed.

YEAST

A British barm seller, 1837

Commercially-made yeast in the form of moist cakes was available to those living in cities beginning in the 1870s. But because fresh yeast is perishable and icebox and root cellar refrigeration needed to keep the yeast active was inconsistent, commercial yeast wouldn't become a kitchen staple until the 1920s. Before the 1920s, American women favored hops-yeast to raise their breads. Here's a typical hops-yeast recipe from Mrs. Mary Randolph's 1833 cook book, *The Virginia Housewife:*

ANOTHER METHOD FOR MAKING YEAST.

Peel one large Irish potato, boil it till soft, rub it through a sieve; add an equal quantity of flour, make it sufficiently liquid with hop tea; and when a little warmer than new milk, add a gill of good yeast; stir it well, and keep it closely covered in a small pitcher.

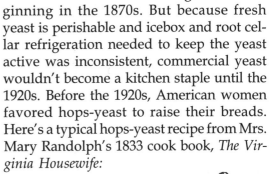

I know, you're wondering just where does that gill of good yeast come from and why bother making hops-yeast when you already have good yeast? And why not just ferment the yeast that lives on your flour for goodness sakes? After reading about a trillion similar yeast recipes, I think I'm starting to figure it out.

Much to the horror of the followers of the temperance movement of the 1830s, it turns out that beer-making and bread making are soul mates. The yeast that ferments the both of them is the same. Leaven, or sourdough, produces a sour product when not tended to regularly and there is much written about the American detestation for foul and injurious sour bread. As L. D. Chapin writes in 1843, *"The use of barm yeast was a great improvement over sour leaven. It is the foam collected on the surface of beer in fermentation. Yeast is now made with hops and malt."*

So I took a little virtual trip back to 18th century Scotland and learned about how to make a Scottish barm, malt hops-yeast. My local beer store provided me with hops, whole malted barley and some ale yeast.

YEAST

First, I boiled two handfuls of hops in two quarts of water for 30 minutes, then I poured the strained hops tea over a cup of unhulled malted barley that I cracked in my hand-cranked grain mill. Once that mixture cooled down, I added enough organic, unbleached flour to make a batter, then added about four specks of brewers yeast. The mixture went into a plastic wrap covered half-gallon jar, and after two days, the flour settled on the bottom topped with brown malt water, crowned by foamy, seething, man-eating yeast. I scooped off some of the floating yeast and made a well-risen, horrible, bitter bread.

Not being one to give up, I made a hops and malt spiked wild yeast sourdough starter that, after being lovingly clucked over for a couple weeks, also made horrible bitter bread.

What I have learned is that hops preserve the yeast that is fed by the starches in both potato and flour. (Malt is a whole other story.) You can add a little of your old yeast to the hops-potato mixture, let it work a day or two and then cork up several jars of dormant yeast which can then be stored in a cool place for months. I also learned that the best leaven is made only from good water and the yeasts that live on your flour. I'll tell you how to make a wild yeast sourdough bread on page 34.

But if you're adventurous like I am, then try Mrs. Randolph's potato hops-yeast on the facing page, with a bit of added instruction from Maria Parloa's, 1872 *Appledore Cook Book*:

"Set the mixture to rise where it will be warm. It will rise in five hours if the yeast is good. You can tell when it is risen by the white foam, which will rise to the top. When risen, put it in a stone jug, and stop tight. It is a good plan to tie the cork down, as it sometimes flies out."

Indeed, my starter has overflowed often, even while refrigerated. I advise you to store yours in a wide-mouth mason jar with plenty of room to expand, covered loosely with plastic wrap.

STORE-BOUGHT YEAST

A re there animaecules in your bread? You'd better hope so! We've come a long way since Antony van Leeuwenhoek's 17th century discovery of yeasts. But figuring out how to get those little fellers to rise our breads the way we want them to can be vexing. Here's a boiled-down version of what you need to know in order to reproduce the historic breads in this book:

YEAST FOR THE HOME BAKER:

Active dry contains 2¼ tsp. per packet. It needs to be hydrated in water in order to get perky.

Instant (also called rapid-rise) has a coating on it that allows it to be combined with dry ingredients. You need 25% less of this yeast to match the raising power of active dry. For the recipes in this book, I have used instant yeast. I prefer the SAF brand, available at organic markets and at online stores. So if you're using active dry, add 25% more yeast than I call for in a recipe.

Fresh yeast is quite perishable and therefore, we home bakers don't see much of it anymore. However, vintage recipes from the 1870s thru the mid-1900s will often call for "yeast cakes." One yeast cake is equal to 1 Tbs. of active dry yeast or 2¼ tsp. of instant yeast.

One cup of good yeast called for in historic recipes is variable. Generally 1 cup water plus either 1 Tbs. active dry yeast or 2¼ tsp. instant yeast.

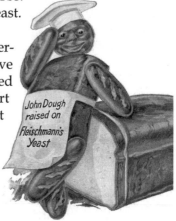

John Dough raised on Fleischmann's Yeast

All that said, I use as little commercial yeast in my breads as possible. I love the flavor and texture of breads raised with wild yeasts. But when I'm short on the time, I make an overnight sponge with water, flour and a very small amount of added yeast, as did most 19th century bread bakers. Once you start sponging, you'll never go back to straight-doughing (same day mixing and baking).

SETTING A SPONGE

A sponge is a pre-ferment that contains water, flour and a little yeast. Experience will tell you how much time it takes for your yeast to digest its supper, and at what temperature. A pre-ferment keeps bread fresh longer and improves flavor and texture. Here's Eliza Acton's 1857 sponge:

"Pour the yeast into the hole in the middle of the flour, and stir into it as much of that which lies round it as will make a thick batter. Strew plenty of flour on the top, throw a thick clean cloth over, and set it where the air is warm ... when the yeast has risen and broken through the flour, and bubbles appear in it, you will know that it is ready to be made up into dough."

The sponge "works" overnight in a hole dug out of all the flour that's used in the recipe. Interestingly, when covered with flour, the sponge does not dry out as it ferments.

There are several different types of pre-ferments that match different styles of bread and they vary according to fermentation time and firmness. The style of pre-ferment we will be using in this book is known as a *poolish*, but our great-grandmothers called it a *sponge*. **You can omit the sponge from these recipes as long as you add the sponge ingredients to the dough recipe and double the yeast. Or, you can add a sponge to any of your favorite bread recipes by doing the reverse.**

SETTING YOUR SPONGE

The night before you bake, stir together a scant cup of all-purpose (AP) flour (120g), ½ cup water and a pinch of instant yeast. Really, a pinch, as in a 16th of a tsp. The consistency of the just-mixed sponge should be thin enough to stir, but too thick to pour. Keep the water constant and decrease flour if necessary. Cover with a plate or plastic wrap, and let it sit at room temperature about 10 hours, until it's bubbly but hasn't begun to shrink back down. Add the ripe sponge to your dough or refrigerate up to three days.

MIXING & KNEADING

"Knead your dough until it's smooth and elastic and feels like a baby's behind," is what I learned growing up. Of course, since we're talking about bread, there's no one correct method of dough mixing. If you're making the sorts of breads made by our American grand-mothers, you'll need to knead about 5-10 minutes by hand. Kneading develops the gluten and distributes food and oxygen to the yeast. If you're making an open-crumbed, crackly crusted artisan bread, the dough will be too wet to knead and you will fold the mass in order to build strength.

Remember, don't add more than a whisper of flour to your dough as you knead. If your hands stick, moisten with water be-fore you add more flour to your board. Too much additional flour at this stage will make your bread hard and dry.

How NOT to knead ...

"To Knead Bread ... After the dough is mixed, flour the hands, and, folding the fingers over the thumb, make what is called a fist, and beat and pummel the dough first with one hand, and then the other on every side; work it thus till it ceases to stick to your hands. Much kneading makes bread whiter and finer; bread can, indeed, scarcely be kneaded too much." Arthur's Home Magazine, 1869

A better way to knead ...

"When you put the bread on the board, mix it lightly, and when you begin to knead it, do not press down, but let all your motions be as elastic as possible; knead with the palm of the hand until the dough is a flat cake, then fold, and keep doing this until the dough is smooth and elastic; twenty minutes is the time I have given, but many per-sons can knead the bread in less time, while others will require longer. Practice will teach." Appledore Cook Book, Maria Parloa 1872

MIXING & KNEADING

FOLDING WET DOUGH

If your dough is too wet to knead, you can give it extensibility and strength by periodic folding after the initial mixing. Let's say your dough is a clock as it sits in the bowl. Grab it from underneath 12:00 and lift it as far as it will stretch easily. Now lay that piece into the middle. Do the same at 9:00, 6:00 and 3:00. I fold wet doughs a few times after mixing the ingredients, and then every 30 minutes during the first half of the bulk (first) fermentation. Once you've shaped your bread for the second rise (the *proof*), refrain from folding.

SHAPING YOUR LOAVES

Contrary to William Jago's 1895 advice to *"bash your dough well to prevent holeyness,"* I say handle your risen dough gently when forming your loaves. You don't want to deflate all the hard won carbon dioxide gas bubbles that will help to cook your bread evenly and quickly. Shaping is an art worth studying. A well cast loaf will hold its form and have loft and a good texture.

After the first rise, flatten your dough slightly and then fold it into thirds like you were mailing a letter, only fold each third into the middle. Let the dough rest 15 minutes if you can, and then stretch it into the desired shape, keeping the outside smooth edge on the outside, pinching the ends at the bottom.

SLASHING

Just before your bread goes into the oven, you'll need to give the top of the loaf a few thoughtfully-placed "slashes" in order to give the bread room for expansion. Use a sharp knife, single-edge razor blade or lame (a tool made for this purpose) to give each loaf a few swift cuts at a 45° angle. Next time you're in a bakery, notice the styles of slashes made for various types of breads.

HOME OVEN BAKING

You've set your sponge, mixed and kneaded your bread. It's risen just right and you're ready to bake. Now what? Let's have a huddle about how to bake your bread, depending on what sort of pan you're using and the style of bread you're baking.

If you're using tin or glass bread pans, preheat your oven to the appropriate temperature. You'll need to create some steam so that your bread will be well-risen.

Photo courtesy of Library of Congress

Place an old metal (not nonstick!) cake pan or cast iron frying pan on the oven floor or lowest shelf to preheat. When your bread is ready to bake, slide it onto the middle rack, and (carefully) pour a cup of hot water into the hot pan and close the door.

If you're baking on a stone, then preheat it to 450° for 45 minutes prior to baking. You'll also need to add steam as above.

If you're baking in a cast iron Dutch oven or a ceramic cloche, you'll need to preheat it at 450° for at least 30 minutes. Please, be careful handling these heavy hot pots!!! I heat the top and bottom of the pans separately so I don't have to pull both out of the oven at once. Get the kids out of the kitchen, wear big oven mitts and make sure you are not distracted when you take the hot pots out of the oven. When you're ready to bake, plop your dough into the hot vessel, slash and put in the oven. Replace the lid and bake. The bread will steam until you remove the hot lid after 15 minutes and then it will continue to bake and brown, uncovered, for about 20 more minutes or until it reaches 200° on an instant-read thermometer (available at kitchen stores for about $15).

CAMPFIRE BAKING

OK, we're having fun now! Grab your Dutch oven and let's go camping. (Or head for the campfire ring in your back yard.) The motor-camping movement from the early 1900s produced lots of great how-to camping books with all sorts of creative make-do cooking advice. Overnight un-kneaded breads are perfect for campouts. Make up the dough and place it in your cooler. Take it out to rise a couple hours before you're ready to bake. Here are a couple of homemade ovens that are sure to entertain your family.

Rock-lined Oven *Dig a hole in the ground, preferably on the side of a knoll; line it with rocks, if possible; build a fire of hardwood within it and keep it up for a half hour at least, till the rocks or the surrounding earth is very hot; rake out the coals and ashes, leaving three to four inches of live coals and ash in the bottom. Put in whatever you have to bake, cover with the ashes. A little experience will soon settle the question of baking time.*

Camp Cooking, 1915

Earth-hole Oven *A hole the depth of a small bucket may be dug in the earth and any quantity of sticks should be placed in this hole. The upper rim should have a series of flat stones placed round, so that the center is a kind of small funnel through which the sticks can be inserted, and the smoke and flame exude, but to keep inside as much heat as possible."* *The Camper's Handbook*, 1908

To bake bread in an earth-hole oven, let the fire die down in your pit, keeping some embers in the bottom. Shovel out a few for the top. Put your dough in a small covered pot. (I like the tiny 1-quart Lodge Dutch oven.) Lower it into the hole and cover with the remaining live embers. Cover the hole with a grill so nobody falls in it! Place a large skillet over the grill-topped hole to retain the heat in the earth-hole oven. You can keep your chili warm in the skillet! Check the bread after 30 minutes.

FIREPLACE BREAD

Oh the fun you'll have baking bread in your fireplace! First, you need to get a good fire burning for about two hours. Take out the grate and firedogs and set them aside. Then create the foundation of your fire with two fat, short logs placed parallel with ends pointing toward you. Build your fire on top of these logs. When the embers drop down, you'll be able to easily shovel them out without having to fight burning logs.

Now, take your cast iron pot with feet and a recessed lid (size 8 is good for one loaf of bread) and preheat it as in this photo from the 1930s. Put some coals under your pot on the hearth in  front of the fire, then cover with more coals. Let your pot get good and hot, then gently flip your bread from proofing basket to hot pan. Put the lid on and refresh the coals. Rotate the pan about every ten minutes, then peek inside after about 25 minutes. Too many ashes on top of the pot will damp down the heat, so when adding a new shovelful, scrape off some of the old ashes.

I am sorry to say, but this is the kind of cooking you have to figure out for yourself. If I tell you every little thing to do for each problem you'll no doubt encounter, then you won't have so much fun! Just remember, charred fireplace bread is just fine.

A couple of hints though ... a lid lifter is a wonderful tool. Lodge makes a good one. Final-proof your dough seam-side-up in a floured towel placed inside a bowl. As soon as you flip it into the pot, do your usual slashing so that the dough can expand. High hydration artisan bread doughs can get rubbery crusts when they do all their baking covered. For covered, live-fire baking, start off with unsweetened doughs that are firm enough to knead by hand. Whole-grain breads bake beautifully in coals.

How To Store Bread

Moral Storage of Bread
A Treatise on Bread Making,
Sylvester Graham, 1837

"Do not store your bread in a pantry which perhaps is seldom thoroughly cleansed with hot water and soap, and where the pure air of heaven seldom if ever has a fine circulation. The quality of your bread should be of too much importance to allow of such reprehensible carelessness, not to say sluttishness. And if you will have your bread such as every one ought to desire to have it, you must pay the strictest attention to the cleanliness and sweetness of the place where you keep it. The best bread-makers I have ever known, watch over their bread troughs while their dough is rising, and over their ovens while it is baking, with about as much care and attention as a mother watches over the cradle of her sick child."

USDA Farmer's Bulletin, 1894 advises:

Tie string only once around lengthwise.

showing label through wax-paper.

"On being taken from the oven, bread should be placed on slats or sieves so that the air can circulate about it until it is thoroughly cooled. By that time all the gas and steam which are likely to escape have done so, and the bread may be put away. Some housekeepers wrap their hot bread in cloths, but this is not advisable, not only because it makes the bread taste of the cloth, but also because it shuts the steam up in the loaf and makes it damp and clammy—an excellent medium for cultivating mold."

Aunt Barb says: Store bread in a heavy paper bag or in an old-timey bread box to prevent the excess moisture which causes mold.

Busy Busy Busy

I'm busy," says you. "*I want to make really good bread quick!*" Oh I know, but forget it. Really good bread takes time. While you don't need to be a slave to your bread, the gazillions of little yeasts that rise your dough need time to do their thing and the more they're rushed, the worse your bread will be.

By using pre-ferments, as did your busy great-grandmothers, your yeasts will work while you sleep! The recent popularity of un-kneaded, overnight breads baked in cast iron pots has intro-duced throngs of weary time-strapped and inexperienced bakers to impressive artisan breads that have left them wanting more. If you've fallen in love with no-knead cast iron bread baking, you'll, no doubt, find that 19th century cooks have lots to offer you in terms of technique and flavor. There's a whole world out there of fantastic nearly lost breads that you can bake in great vintage ironware.

Photo courtesy of Library of Congress

I just want to put in one teensy little plug here for making a simpler life for yourself. Sometimes it takes something as unsophisticated as dough to make you take stock of the pace of your life. Dipping your hands in a bowl of bread batter is downright sensuous and the rhythm of kneading and folding and shaping your dough is relaxing. Besides, your bread can tell if you're tense and rushed... hurrying rips up the gluten that holds your bread together leaving you with flaccid, insipid loaves. You don't want that, do you? So when it comes to bread making, it's best to simmer down, make a cup of tea and carve out some time from your busy schedule for you and your dough. Before you know it, you'll be hanging your laundry in the sun to dry and chopping logs to feed your wood cookstove!

Baking-Day

Scheduling Your Bread Bake

You can nudge your bread into your busy schedule by giving it a rest (*retarding*) in the refrigerator during its first or second rise. Retarding dough that includes a sponge can sometimes produce a limp loaf if you use bread flour, so AP is a better choice for this method.

Mid-morning bread: Start your sponge in the morning and mix up your bread after supper. Form into its final shape before bed and refrigerate overnight for a long, cool rise that will add even more flavor to your bread. Let the dough warm to room temperature for about two hours and then bake as directed.

Lunchtime bread: Make a sponge in the morning, mix up your dough in the evening and let it rise in a covered bowl overnight in your fridge. In the morning, let it sit at room temperature about an hour, form it into loaves for the second rise, and it should be ready to bake in about two hours.

Evening workday bread: Start your sponge the night before you bake, mix your bread in the morning and refrigerate before going to work. Bake it in the evening and you'll have fresh bread for a bedtime snack.

Died of Bread Making, *Michigan Farmer,* 1888

"One of my neighbors makes as nice hop yeast bread as I ever saw, but she never seems free from the care and thought of it. As soon as one batch is baked, she begins to make preparations for the next. Her husband said to me: "Bell didn't make as good bread for a while as Martha (his first wife) used to, but I told her more time and attention must be given to the matter, and now, it is all right." Poor girl! she's a slave to making bread for that family of seven, and sometime ere long I shall feel like scribbling on her tombstone, **"Died of bread making."**

BREAD RECIPE WANTED

BREAD RECIPE WANTED
Cultivator and Country Gentleman, 1866

"Is there a person among all your numerous readers who can give me a good, reliable recipe for making bread? I think I have asked nearly every house-keeper of my acquaintance, and the only answer I have been able to get as yet, is, "Oh, my dear sir, I never had any regular recipe for making bread—who ever heard of such a thing? I always make it by guess; that's the way my mother always done, and that's the way every one else does. So much flour, as near as you can guess, so by the eye you know; so much 'emptins (yeast); mix; then let it stand to 'rise' a longer or shorter time; use your judgment you know; chuck it into the oven, and bake until you guess it's done, and you will always have light, sweet, beautiful bread."

A gentleman reader

Poor feller. He's suffering the same fate you're about to, especially if you're new to bread baking or you're used to following recipes. Remember, great bread bakers spend a lifetime learning their craft. It takes as long to get a good understanding of bread baking as it does to learn a new language or play an instrument. Books, videos and personal instruction, together, provide a great start.

Regardless of your baking experience, I hope you'll give these tasty recipes a try, but understand that they are from an era in time when the keepers of the home (a.k.a. women) stayed at home, and the weekly ritual of baking bread was a skill passed down from mother to daughter from a tender age. Don't let your younguns turn out like the exasperated gentleman above; invite your kids and grandkids to join you in your bread making adventures! (Just be sure to shoo them out of the kitchen when handling the hot pots!)

FAMILY BREAD

When I think of old-time family breads, the rustic loaf this woman is holding is what comes to mind. Can't you just see yourself sitting at her hand-hewn table, dunking your crusty hunk of dark bread into your bowl of thick pea soup?

Unfortunately, her loaf has little to do with historic American bread, first of all, because she's French. Besides that little detail, Americans didn't care for coarse peasant breads of this sort back when Désiré François Laugée created this painting in the mid-1800s. For one thing, this farmwife is holding the loaf, which would horrify our American ancestors of gentle birth who ate white, refined wheat manchet rolls in order to minimize handling by the "help." On top of that, Americans detested supposedly sour French breads raised by wild yeast leavens pretty much up until the 1960s when San Francisco sourdough breads became widely popular.

The farmhouse "miche" our French lady is slicing takes a bit of skill to master, so we're going to start off with a lighter version of her bread, leavened with a small amount of commercial yeast. The recipe for *rustic farmhouse bread* begins on page 30.

Rustic farmhouse family bread baked in a preheated clay cloche.

> "The popular machine-made bread is surely to be preferred before hand-made bread, with the possible contingency of contamination from the bodies of the half-naked operatives."
> ~1892 International Congress of Hygiene

FAMILY BREAD

HOW TO COOK WITHOUT A BOOK

I'm going to show you how to bake bread by the seat of your pants, great-grandmother style. Professional bakers use a "baker's percentage" in order to bake their various breads. They weigh the flour and everything else (liquid, salt, yeast, etc.) is a percentage of the flour's weight. In my kitchen, I also use this formula if I'm baking an artisan style loaf with flour I've not used before so I can keep track of what I tried. But here's how I learned to bake bread, and it works pretty darn well most of the time. And, it's about the only way I know of to decipher an historic recipe.

I look for how much liquid is in a recipe and then I add 1 tsp. of salt for each cup of water or milk. Then, I know that each cup of liquid will need about 2½ cups of flour, depending on dough hydration, whole grains, etc. One-half tsp. of instant yeast will raise one cup of liquid's worth of bread if you use an overnight sponge. One cup of liquid will make one regular size loaf of bread. If baking in a 5-quart pan, then "half-again" the entire recipe. That's pretty much it. Ok, let's take this method for a spin.

RUSTIC FARMHOUSE FAMILY BREAD

This recipe makes one loaf of simple bread with a crunchy crust and an open-ish crumb. We'll start off with a light bread and then I'll give suggestions for other styles to suit your family's tastes.

Evening sponge (see page 19):
   ½ cup water, 1 scant cup AP flour (120g), pinch instant yeast
Dough:
   ½ cup water   ½ tsp. instant yeast
   1 tsp. fine salt   1½ cups AP (all purpose) flour (195g)

The night before you bake, make your sponge. In the morning, add water to the sponge and mix well. Stir in one cup flour mixed with the salt and the yeast and stir. Then add flour until you have a mixture that is almost dry enough to knead. Cover the bowl and let it sit for 30 minutes.

If you have a stand mixer, knead for about 3 minutes on speed 2 until the dough clears the sides but still sticks just a bit on the bottom. By hand, knead about 5-10 minutes, adding as little flour as possible to get the job done, until the ball of dough is smooth.

FAMILY BREAD

Rustic Farmhouse Bread Continued ...

Now, take that ball of dough and place it in a buttered bowl to rise. Cover the bowl with a plate. Let rise until doubled, about 2 hours. Gently, without totally deflating, stretch dough into a round shape, pinching seams at the bottom. Place in a flour-dusted towel set into a bowl good-side-down. Let the dough rise again, covered with an inverted bowl or in a large plastic bag, until doubled, about 90 minutes. Forty-five minutes before you're ready to bake, preheat your oven and baking stone, Dutch oven, or cloche to 450°. CAREFULLY, remove the pan from the oven and dump your dough into it. Slash three times down the center and bake 15 minutes with the lid on. Remove the lid and bake about 15 more minutes until dark brown, about 200° on an instant-read thermometer. If baking on a stone or in a bread pan, you'll need to add steam by pouring a cup of hot water into a hot cake pan placed in the bottom of your oven when the bread goes in.

HOW TO TELL IF YOUR DOUGH HAS RISEN ENOUGH

The first rise is called the bulk fermentation, the second rise is called the "proof." To tell if your dough is proofed enough to bake, poke it. If the dough springs back quickly, it's not ready. If it springs back slowly, then it's perfect. No spring at all, probably overproofed , but bake it anyway.

Peasant loaf baked in a 1940s 5-qt. cast iron Dutch oven that I found at a yard sale for $25.

Peasant Style Farmhouse Bread - For a mid-morning whole grain version of the farm-house bread, replace ½ to 1 cup of the white flour with a mixture of rye and/or whole wheat. Set the sponge in the morning, mix the dough early evening, forming into a loaf be-fore bed. Place on a baking sheet, seam side down, cover, and refrigerate overnight. Next morning, let dough come to room temperature about two hours and then bake as above.

*Note: When substituting whole grain flour, add a splash more liquid per cup as whole grains absorb more liquid than refined flours. Bread flours also absorb more liquid than do lower-gluten all purpose flours.

FAMILY BREAD

OVERNIGHT UN-KNEADED BREAD

Here's a flat-out easy and darn good way to make a large loaf of bread that'll give you good practice for the other radiant heat baked breads in this book. This un-kneadably wet dough rises overnight to be baked in a 5-quart hot cast iron or ceramic pot the following mid-morning. Most 19th century whole grain breads were made in this fashion. Start with un-bleached flour and then progress to whole grains. And have your wits about you when you make this bread in HOT pans! Shoo the kids out of the kitchen when handling the pot.

Morning Sponge **(see page 19):**
     ½ cup water, 1 scant cup AP flour (120g), pinch instant yeast

Evening Dough:
2¾ cups unbleached AP (all purpose) flour (357g)
½ cup (65g) whole wheat or rye flour   1¾ tsp. fine salt
Pinch instant yeast   1¼ cups water

In the morning, set your sponge. In the evening, make your dough. Into a large bowl, measure out your flours and stir in the salt and yeast. Add the water, sponge and stir, stir, stir. Cover and let it sit about 10 hours. When dough is nice and puffy, place it on a floured board and try to form it into a ball by stretching sides and pinching them in at the bottom. Don't squish the air out of your dough as you work. It will be quite wet and sticky. Now get a smooth surfaced kitchen towel, rub lots of flour into it, and put it in a bowl that's about twice the size of your dough. Place your dough in the towel-lined bowl, seam side up and let it rise about 90 minutes. It should rise by a half. If available, sprinkle cornmeal on top.

Meanwhile, 45 minutes before you expect to bake, place your 5-quart cast iron Dutch oven, lid on, in a 450° oven. When the dough has risen as instructed above, dump it into the HOT pan, put the lid on, and place it back in the oven. Some dough will stick to the towel, just pry it off. It adds character to your bread. Bake for 15 minutes, then remove lid and continue to bake another 25 or so minutes until loaf is a very dark golden brown.

FAMILY BREAD

In bygone days, bakers would sprinkle flour or cornmeal over the sponge. The sponge had finished working when the cornmeal "cracked". We're using the same technique as we sprinkle cornmeal on top of the dough for the final rise. When you flip the bread into the pan, the cornmeal forms a crunchy crust on the bottom of your bread.

OVERNIGHT UN-KNEADED WHOLE GRAIN BREAD

Use up to 2 cups of your favorite whole grain flour in place of the white. Add one Tbs. more water per cup of unbolted (whole grain) flour.

OVERNIGHT UN-KNEADED PIZZA DOUGH

If you like pizza with a chewy crust and moist holey crumb, this dough will be your new best friend. Prepare the overnight un-kneaded bread dough. After the first rise, form it into two balls and let them rest in the refrigerator up to 2 days. When ready to bake, let the chilled dough sit at room temperature a couple hours, and then gently stretch each ball into the shape of your pizza stone. 45 minutes before you bake, turn the oven to 500° and preheat your pizza stone. Place the flattened dough on a piece of parchment paper that's been sprinkled with cornmeal, lay on your toppings, then slide into hot oven to bake. You can slip the parchment off after the crust has firmed and continue to bake until brown and bubbly.

OVERNIGHT CHEESE BREAD

This bread is so good and easy to make, it's almost not fair. Roughly chop 6 oz. good white sharp cheddar and mix it in with your dough ingredients. If your dough doesn't tear from being stuck to the towel when dumping it into the hot pan to bake, give it a couple slashes. Sometimes, I just place grated cheese in a big pile in the middle of the dough as I'm forming it into a ball to go into the bowl for the second rise. It explodes out the top when it bakes like a big baked crunchy cheese volcano.

WILD YEAST BREAD

We know wild yeast leavened breads as "sourdough," today, but your great-grandmother called them "self-working" yeast breads. And she probably didn't like them because neglected starters make sour, off-tasting breads and busy housewives a hundred years ago had no patience for that.

Sourdough bread is made using yeasts that live in the air, on your hands, and, best of all, on the grains that you use to bake your breads. Although these undomesticated bacteria that lift your breads thrive in the acidic environment created by fermenting grains, your breads won't taste sour unless your yeasts are underfed. Well-tended starters produce fragrant breads that have an open crumb and a chewy but crisp and tasty crust with a relatively long shelf-life.

Professional bakers who write bread books tend to be rather dogmatic about how to create and bake with a starter, but we home bakers don't need to be so persnickety if we're just baking a couple loaves a week.

WILD YEAST SEED CULTURE

Day 1: Into a wide-mouth quart canning jar, mix ¼ cup filtered, unchlorinated water, ¼ cup (preferably organic) AP flour and 1 Tbs. rye flour (can substitute white flour, but rye loves to ferment). Cover lightly with plastic wrap and leave at room temperature 24 hours.
Metric weights are approximately 56g. water, 40g. flour.
A couple times each day, give your culture a vigorous stir to aerate.
Day 2: Stir in an additional ¼ cup water, ¼ cup flour plus 1 Tbs. rye.
Day 3: Same.
Day 4: You should have a bubbly seed culture that smells yeasty. Once you've reached this point, feed twice a day starting with 1 Tbs. of culture and ¼ cup flour plus 1 Tbs. of either AP, rye, or whole wheat flour. (I know, it's disheartening to dispose of your remaining seed culture, but it's not ready to work just yet.)
Day 5: Same as day 4
Day 6: Continue day 4 feeding schedule until a dab of your unstirred culture floats in water. At this point, you're ready to turn it into a "starter" culture and start baking.

WILD YEAST BREAD

FROM SEED CULTURE TO STARTER

Now that your seed culture floats, you're ready to plump it up for baking, usually around day 7 or 8. From now on, you will have to tend to your seed culture by feeding (refreshing) it regularly and either baking with it or putting it to sleep in the fridge. Your seed culture becomes a "starter" once it begins eating equal weights of flour and water. Your starter wants to be fed the same food on a regular schedule, so if you bake often, you can keep it alive on your countertop and feed thus:

Twice a day, mix 1 Tbs. of starter with 50 g. each of organic AP flour and filtered water, (about ¼ cup water and ⅓ cup plus 1 Tbs. AP flour)

I don't save the remaining starter because it's not up to speed for about two weeks. After two weeks of feeding, you can refrigerate your starter instead of refreshing daily. It's painful and wasteful to throw away good ingredients if you only bake once a week or so. When refrigerated, your starter must be refreshed once a week by feeding it on the above schedule, or by baking bread. One day's feeding should suffice. If you're not baking, refrigerate your starter once it starts to bubble after feeding, in order to keep it strong. Now, we're ready to bake. On the following two pages, we'll make the same sourdough bread on two schedules.

Sesame Sourdough

"LEAVEN is nothing more nor less than flour and water, stirred together and kept in a warm place until fermentation commences. The use of leaven is supposed to have originated in Egypt. It is very seldom used in this country now, but sailors use it on long voyages. The bread made from it has always a rank, sour taste, and is not to be compared with yeast-made."

The New System of Making Bread, 1903

EGYPTIANS CARRYING GRAIN TO THE THRESHING FLOOR.

WILD YEAST BREAD

Your starter is ready to bake with if it floats 5 hours after feeding. If not, you will want to feed it twice a day until it's ready. I recommend letting the dough for this recipe rise in a clear glass bowl so you can track the formation of the gas bubbles. Don't tell your holey-bread-hating grandmothers, but more bubbles equals an open-crumbed bread, which is your goal. This flavorful rustic loaf should have a deeply darkened, blistered crust with tender, chewy innards. High gluten bread flour will give you a chewy crumb and crust. AP flour will give you a softer crumb and crispy crust. I recommend using AP flour, you'll have a higher rise. If you bake sourdough breads, go ahead and spring for a scale.

PREPARING FOR MID-MORNING BAKED BREAD

For those of you who work during the week, here's a bread that won't take up your whole weekend. This bread will go into the oven 1-2 hours after you pull it from your fridge in the morning. Let's say we want bread for Saturday lunch ...

Thursday evening: To 1 Tbs. of starter, you will stir in 50g (¼ cup) water and 50g (scant ½ cup) AP flour. Cover with plastic wrap and leave it out at room temperature. Keep the remaining unfed back-up starter in the fridge in case there's some problem with your new feeding.

Friday morning: Add 50g water and 50g flour.

Before dinner on Friday afternoon, mix up your dough using 150g of your fed, plumpy starter. (Approx. ¾ cup unstirred starter.)

The remaining starter gets fed 50g. water and 50g. of flour and then 3 hours later as it's getting bubbly, you refrigerate it for your next batch of bread. Now you can give away or dispose of the small amount of old back-up starter in your fridge.

Author's note: You can adjust this bread to your schedule, just remember to feed the starter at least twice, then mix your dough. The bulk fermentation (first rise) will take 4-5 hours, the proof (second rise) should take around 2-3 hours if the dough is about 76°. I find that the dough is less sour if you retard it in the refrigerator on the second rise rather than the first, and less sour, still, if it's baked all in one day.

WILD YEAST BREAD

RUSTIC COUNTRY WILD YEAST BREAD

¾ cup(150g) plumped starter   1¾ tsp. fine salt (10g)
1½ cup (336g) water   3 cups (390g) AP flour
1 cup (130g) whole wheat, rye or AP (all purpose) flour

Combine the starter and water and then add the flours and salt. Stir well and let the mixture rest, covered with a plate or plastic wrap for one hour. Knead with mixer 1 minute or by hand a few minutes and return to the covered bowl. Add as little additional flour during kneading as possible, the dough will be rather soft. If you can, give it a round of folds every 30 minutes or so for the first hour, otherwise, just let it be for about 4-5 hours until it has doubled in size and is full of bubbles. Now, form into two small loaves or one big round loaf and place on a cornmeal dusted piece of parchment paper placed on a cookie sheet in your fridge. Cover with a bowl. In the morning, let the dough come to room temperature about 1-2 hours and if it seems well proofed (dough springs back slowly when poked), slash and bake it in a very hot preheated oven.

If baking in a cast iron pan or a ceramic cloche, proof overnight in a covered flour-dusted cloth-lined bowl. Preheat pan in 475° oven and bake covered 20 minutes. Remove cover and continue to bake until quite brown and the internal temperature reaches 200°, about 20 to 30 more minutes.

If baking on a pizza stone, preheat the stone in a 475° oven and place a pan for steam in the bottom of the oven. Put your bread that's still on the room temperature cookie sheet into the oven, along with a cup of hot water in your steam pan. After about 10 minutes, you can slide the bread off the cookie sheet and continue to bake it on the stone until done.

If baking on a cookie sheet, follow the directions for the pizza stone.

Author's note: If your loaf does not hold its shape in the overnight rise, next time proof seam-side-up in a floured cloth-lined bowl. In the meantime, give it a stretch and tuck and then let rise at least 2 hours before baking.

WHOLE GRAIN BREADS

Pull on your wellies and let's take a quick skip back in time to Wales for a lesson in crafting early 19th century brown "pot" breads. First, a quick stop at the ale house for some brewer's barm yeast. Now, on to the countryside where those among us of "gentle birth" are to be given instruction by a 93 year old Welsh hermit in the matter of practical cookery.

What follows are some excerpts and a couple of bread recipes from a clever book called, "*Good Cookery Illustrated*," written by Augusa Llanover in 1867. In the book, she spins a tale of a "traveller" from London who stumbles upon an aged Welshman who lives in a primitive house cut from rock that sits next to a limpid spring-fed pool. The kindly hermit knows a bit of everything that nature has to teach but has never ventured forth into the "modern" world, until the traveller drags him to London at the end of the book. Anyway, the traveller and the hermit teach each other about foraging, hunting, farming and the preparation of the various wild and domesticated foods in each others' lives.

Of course, the hermit is quite the prophet and his timeless wisdom about making a simpler life aimed at the "genteel" folks for which the book is written isn't lost on the overextended reader of today. And with that, I present you with the hermit's method for preparing "pot bread" which I know you will just love, along with an awesome apple bread recipe.

The Hermit and the Traveller

BROWN BREAD

BROWN BREAD. *"The brown bread, or household bread of old times, is now hardly to be met with, and is rare even in Wales, the reason being that the millers do*

not grind and prepare the flour in the same way as formerly, when the pure corn (wheat kernel), having been sent to be ground, was returned by the miller with the bran and flour altogether; and in every house there was a good-wife or widow, who sifted the flour required for each baking, removing only the large flake bran. Bread thus made is very superior in flavour to the bread now generally used, but where the above plan cannot be followed, it is best to mix fresh sifted bran with the flour. The flavour of bread is in the bran."

Good Cookery Illustrated, 1867

WELSH PAN OR POT BREAD, 1867

I wanted to call this book *Pot Breads,* but my kids convinced me otherwise. Probably a good idea, but this Welsh pot bread, also from *Good Cookery Illustrated,* is what I had in mind.

"Take three pounds and a half of brown flour (flour which has only had the coarser bran taken out of it), put it to rise with two table-spoonfuls of barm, and, when risen, mix it and knead it in the usual manner; then put it into an iron pot or a thick earthen pan, and turn it topsy-turvy on a flat stone, which should be placed on the ground in the middle of a heap of hot embers, made by burning wood, peat, or turf; cover the pot or pan entirely over with hot embers, leave it to bake, and when the ashes are cold take it out. This mode of baking produces most excellent bread."

Recipe right from *Uncle Sam's 1917 Advice to Housewives.*

> ### HOME-GROUND WHEAT BREAD
>
> | 1¼ cups water or skim milk. | 3 cups home-ground wheat |
> | 1¼ teaspoons salt. | flour. |
> | 1 tablespoon sugar. | ½ cake dry yeast or 1 gill of liquid yeast. |
>
> Set a sponge at night, using half of the flour. In the morning add the rest of the flour, beat well, put into a greased pan, allow to rise until it doubles its bulk, and bake.

BROWN BREAD

APPLE BROWN BREAD
Good Cookery Illustrated, 1867

"Boil twelve apples till soft; core and peel them, break them up, and pulp through a sieve; put sugar to taste, and mix them with twice its weight of dough, and bake them in a very slow oven."

Apple Parer.

I'm excited about this bread of French origin. I first saw it mentioned in a British farming magazine from 1821. Cooked, dried apples stood in where wheat would have resided on account of a poor wheat harvest. Apples were swapped for wheat in a proportion of 1 part apple to 3 parts flour. American whole grain bread activist, R.T. Trall, published an updated version in his 1867 *Hygienic Health Magazine*. Here's a tweaked rendition of his recipe. The flavor of the apples is subtle but the fragrance that wafts through the air as the bread bakes will send you swooning. It makes fantastic french toast. My chef friend, Mark, who tested the recipe, recommends pairing it with an aromatic cheese or baked beans. Don't succumb to the temptation to add cinnamon. It inhibits the action of the yeast and covers up the flavor of the apples. You'll need 6 medium-sized apples.

Evening Sponge (see page 19):
   ½ cup water, 1 cup (120g) AP flour, pinch instant yeast
Dough:

Sponge	2 cups (260g) whole wheat flour
2 cups (450g)cooked apples	1 cup (130g) AP flour
3 Tbs. honey	1 cup (130g) AP flour, reserved
2 tsp. fine salt	1 tsp. instant yeast

The night before you bake, make your sponge. Next day, peel, core, slice 6 interesting tart apples. I like Gold Rush apples. They hold their shape and fall apart all at the same time and taste great, but any apple will do. Cook them almost to a sauce with no more than ¼ cup of either cider, Calvados (apple brandy) or water. Let cool until just warm.

See next page.....

BROWN BREAD

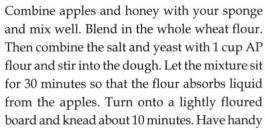

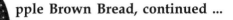

Apple Brown Bread, continued ...

Combine apples and honey with your sponge and mix well. Blend in the whole wheat flour. Then combine the salt and yeast with 1 cup AP flour and stir into the dough. Let the mixture sit for 30 minutes so that the flour absorbs liquid from the apples. Turn onto a lightly floured board and knead about 10 minutes. Have handy your remaining cup of flour. As you knead, the apples will release their juices. Add a sprinkling of your flour, as needed, until you have a nice smoothish dough. Place in a covered buttered bowl to rise until doubled, at least 2 hours. Divide into two pieces. Gently shape the dough into round loaves to be baked in either a Dutch oven or on a baking stone. This bread also does quite well in bread pans. Let the loaves rise, about 2 hours, until nearly doubled. (See page 31, "How to tell if your dough has risen enough.")

Slash the top a few times and then bake in preheated 400° oven around 30 minutes until browned and the internal temperature is 200° on an instant-read thermometer. If you bake in bread pans or on a baking stone, add steam by pouring a cup of hot water into a preheated cast iron frying pan or cake pan on bottom shelf of the oven.

Note: This apple bread is happy with a long, slow rise. You can refrigerate the just-mixed dough overnight, and then form into loaves and bake the following day. Or, once you've formed your loaves, refrigerate them overnight and then bring to room temperature about two hours before baking.

CINNAMON TOAST (FRENCH TOAST)
Cook Book, Debbie Coleman, 1855

"Cut some bread in slices, not too thick and dip them into a mixture of egg, milk and sugar in the proportions of custards but do not cook it. Fry in butter, and serve on a plate dusted with cinnamon."

MIXED GRAIN BREADS

While 18th century early Americans of "means" were pecking at soft fine-grained rolls made from white bolted wheat, everybody else was making do with rustic breads made from locally grown and milled mixed grains. Those coarse loaves of the working class would later become the darlings of the early 19th century health foods movement. By the mid-1800s, mixed-grain breads graced the tables of wealthy and poor alike, though unbolted wheat of decent quality was scarce for those without access to a trustworthy neighborhood grist mill.

Nineteenth century American brown breads were most often a hearty mixture of corn and rye sweetened with molasses, or occasionally, pumpkin. These so-called rye and Indian breads (corn was known as "Indian meal" up until around 1920) are an acquired taste, but here's a recipe you can play with. It's from a late 19th century article on early American breads. If your bread gets too dark baking in the oven, well heck, just make coffee out of it!

RYE N' INDIAN
New England Kitchen Magazine, 1895

"Scald one cup corn meal with one quart boiling milk, and let it cook fifteen minutes, add two tablespoons molasses, one teaspoon salt and let it cool; meanwhile dissolve one ounce of yeast in two table-spoons water, and beat thoroughly into the cornmeal batter; mix in three cups of rye meal, not flour; if very coarse sift out some of the bran, but keep three cups to mix with, put into an iron pan, bake in a sponge cake oven, but let it stay in two hours at least, covering closely if there is danger of browning. The old way was to put it in for the last baking of the brick oven and let it stand all night. If the upper crust was too hard it was evenly sliced from the loaf, well browned and used for crust coffee or brewis, either of which needs only to be known to be appreciated."

Note: "One ounce yeast" would have been a fresh yeast cake and a "sponge cake oven" is a slow oven, 300° or so. I'd bake this bread at 375°.

Mixed Grain Breads

Corn Bread
The Housekeeper, August 1880

"To two quarts of meal, add one pint of bread sponge; water enough to wet the whole. Add one-half pint of flour, and a tablespoonful of salt. Let it rise, and place the dough in the oven, and allow it to bake one hour and a half. This recipe took the first premium, offered at the office of American Agriculturist."

—Corn or Maize

Honey Cornmeal Bread

This beloved, buttery-tasting moist bread (based on the above recipe) is simple to make and is best when fresh and warm. It's my new favorite housewarming gift bread. If possible, use a good, fresh-ground yellow cornmeal from your local grist mill. If you don't live near a grist mill, try Bob's Red Mill stoneground cornmeal found at organic markets and grocery stores nationwide.

Evening sponge (see page 19):
    1 cup water, scant 2 cups (240g) AP flour, big pinch instant yeast
Dough:

1 cup boiling water	1¾ tsp. fine salt
1 cup fresh cornmeal	1 tsp. instant yeast
Up to 2½ cups (325g) AP flour	2 Tbs. honey

The night before, prepare your sponge. In a separate bowl, pour 1 cup boiling water over 1 cup cornmeal. Stir well and cover. In the morning, combine soaked cornmeal, the sponge and honey and mix well. Stir in yeast, salt and 2¼ cups flour. Let the dough rest 30 minutes and then knead 5 minutes by hand or a few minutes in mixer on speed 2 until smooth. Add as little additional flour as necessary so that you can knead the dough without it sticking to the board. It should be quite sticky. Place in buttered bowl. Cover and let rise until doubled, about 90 minutes to 2 hours. Form into two loaves and place in generously buttered loaf pans. Let rise, covered, until nearly doubled, about 90 minutes. Slash the top three times across and bake in preheated 400° oven for 35 minutes or until internal temperature is 200° and bread is nicely browned.

MIXED GRAIN BREADS

Rye bread is brainy, evocative, honest and edgy. It's simple, rustic, ethnic, familiar and curious and just so darn interesting. You can spend your whole life reconstructing the elusive rye bread of your past. My own dear father has the rye bread monkey on his back (see page 58) and so does Molly in the following story-recipe from *Good Housekeeping*, 1886.

Orange Currant Rye Bread

GERMAN RYE BREAD, 1886

"Molly knew the virtues of rye bread, and in perfection, as she had eaten it once in her life, she had enjoyed it much, it had been so sweet. She knew that to some people rye bread represented a texture that cut like liver, that was sweet in flavor, but in wheaten bread would have been called heavy, and to others it was a sour, dark bread, much approved by Germans. But that rye bread need be neither of these she knew well, but she had no recipe."

"On thinking it over she couldn't see why rye bread should not be made in the same way as white. Finally she went to work to make it exactly as white bread, making a sponge with a pint of white flour and half a cake of yeast, dissolved in a pint of warm water, a tablespoonful of sugar and two teaspoonfuls of salt. When this was as full of holes as honeycomb, she put to it two pints of rye flour and used as much warm water as would make all into a soft dough. She kneaded it, but began to understand why it was usually stirred, for it stuck to her hands like bird-lime* and to use flour enough to free them, she knew would spoil her bread. She worked on, regardless of stickiness, and when it was mixed, divided the dough in three, put it in tins to rise and when each was double the first size, they were baked in a very moderate oven one hour. When they were done Molly saw she had attained the secret of her friend's bread, for it was sweet, spongy, and with a tender crust."

*Bird-lime was a sticky substance used to trap birds in Molly's day. If you make this recipe, remember to keep track of your liquid, and adjust salt to 1 tsp. per cup of water.

Mixed Grain Breads

Orange Currant Rye

This hearty, orange perfumed bread'll make you want to put on a red flannel shirt and chop a big pile of wood. Use the best grains you can find and serve thin slices with an uncomplicated cheese. When made with a sourdough culture, rye bread tastes and holds its shape better. If you have a sourdough starter, replace the pinch of yeast with a tsp. of starter in the overnight sponge. Be fore-warned: Your dough will be delightfully sticky to knead! This recipe makes one large loaf, best baked in a 5-quart Dutch oven.

Evening Sponge (see page 19):
  ½ cup water, 1 scant cup bread flour (120g), pinch instant yeast
Dough:

Sponge	1½ tsp. fine salt
1 cup water	1½ tsp. instant yeast

1 cup (130g) bread flour
2 cups (260g) rye flour (half whole wheat is also good)
1 cup currants soaked in 3 Tbs. Cointreau or other orange liqueur
1 Tbs. orange marmalade, chopped or zest of one orange (optional)

The night before you bake, set your sponge. In a separate bowl, soak the currants in the liqueur (or orange juice). Next day, combine sponge, water, marmalade, the flours, yeast and salt. Stir well and let mixture rest for 30 minutes. With your hands, squish in the drained currants and knead 10 minutes by hand or 4 minutes by machine on speed 2. Add just enough flour to be able to knead (depending on flour, could be ¼ cup additional). Let the dough rise in a covered bowl until doubled, 2-3 hours. Form into a ball and let rise again good-side-down, in a flour dusted towel set inside a bowl, about 1½ -2 hours. Preheat oven to 425° along with cloche or Dutch oven. Flip dough into your pan. Bake covered for 15 minutes, then remove cover and bake 20 more minutes or until 200° on instant-read thermometer.

Rye Bread, 1869—"Rye bread is made the same as wheat; it is troublesome on account of the rye sticking to your hands. Use a little wheat flour on them."

MIXED GRAIN BREADS

Thirded breads, consisting of equal parts of coarsely ground graham-style wheat, cornmeal and rye, were the homespun breads of the Colonial-era common man. From the Mid-South and especially into New England, these mixed grain breads were routinely found on American dinner tables until after World War I. Thirded breads were either baked or steamed, each method producing a distinctly different product. Both are toothsome and as good as the grains used to prepare them. The Boston brown bread which survives to this day, is an example of a steamed thirded bread leavened with baking soda. Though thirded breads were traditionally sweetened with molasses or sorghum syrup (depending on whether you lived in the North or the South), the welcome debut of raisins is a more recent addition.

THIRD BREAD
Aunt Mary's New England
Cook Book, 1881

Are these directions below great or what? I tried this recipe as written, and to be honest, although it tastes good, it's not a pretty bread. To be authentic, I ground my grains in my hand-cranked mill. The coarse grind of graham flour that would have been used in the recipe, slices through what little gluten is in the dough. That makes for a heavy loaf that even the perkiest yeast can't lift. Let me just say that when you eat this bread, you know you've eaten it. I'm not messing with this recipe, especially the "mix with warm water until the spoon comes out smooth" part. It's just too good as written.

A POST MILL.

"To a pint each of wheat and rye flour and corn meal add two tablespoons of molasses; one half cake of compressed yeast; mix with warm water until the spoon comes out smooth; rise over night, and again while in the pans before baking."

Mixed Grain Breads

Sour Milk Steamed (Boston) Brown Bread

Mrs. Lincoln's Boston Cook-Book, 1896

You are going to love this flavorful "modern" version of a Colonial-era steamed thirded bread. This 1896 recipe is great, and needs very little tweaking. Use the freshest, best tasting flours you can get your hands on, and slather the moist, dark, round slices with cream cheese. Wrapped well, it stays moist for several days.

1 cup of corn meal	*1 teaspoon soda (scant)*
1 cup of rye flour	*½ cup molasses*
1 cup Graham flour	*1 pint sour milk (buttermilk)*
1 teaspoon (fine) salt	*1 cup stoned (seeded) raisins*

"Mix the meal with flour. Mash the soda and salt before measuring; sift and mix thoroughly with the flour; add the sour milk and molasses, and beat well. If not moist enough to pour, add a little warm water. Pour it into a well-greased mould or pail, filling it only two thirds full. Cover it with a tight cover, also greased. Steam three hours in a steamer, or set the pail in a kettle of boiling water. Keep the water boiling; and as it boils away, replenish with boiling water to keep it at the same level. Remove the cover, and place the mould in the oven fifteen minutes to dry the crust."

Updated Brown Bread

Add 1 teaspoon of baking powder to the dry ingredients, and **an optional tablespoon brown sugar or orange marmalade** to the batter. Use sorghum syrup (available at farm markets in the South) or good molasses. Never bitter blackstrap molasses! Butter four wide-mouthed pint canning jars, coffee cans, or mini loaf pans, etc. Fill jars ¾ full and put a piece of foil over the top. Place jars in a baking pan filled with water (about a third of the way up the jars) in a 350° oven for an hour. Then, remove the foil and continue to bake another 15 minutes to dry the crust a bit. Flip the jars over onto a cookie sheet, and bake another few minutes until brown on the bottom. Slide cakes out to cool on a metal rack.

GEMS

Do you have an iron gem pan in your pantry? I'm guessing not. Unless perhaps, you're a collector of antique cast ironware, and then, it might be hanging on the wall by your fireplace. In my official poll of about a gazillion people who cook, tragically, not one had ever baked a gem muffin in an antique gem pan. Graham gems were in just about every single recipe book up until the 1930s, and most every American kitchen contained at least one type of cast iron gem pan. How these dear little health breads have managed to vanish so completely from our lives is a mystery. Therefore, I am starting a gem revolution. Right here and now.

Whole grain gems came into popularity in the 1860s, following the 1830s health food craze initiated by Sylvester Graham. Fortunately, the popularity of his graham, unbolted wheat flour breads outlasted his rather extremist moral ideology. Graham advocated a plant based diet that included "entire wheat" flour, abstention from alcohol as well as putting the kibosh on romantic frolicking for pretty much everybody. Hence, Graham's untimely undoing. His namesake "graham" flour, however, survived and would be found in American flour bins for the next hundred years.

While graham breads were also known as "dyspepsia" breads, thanks to the fiber's action on ailing guts, graham gems were the descendants of early 1800s breakfast drop cakes that were baked in shallow tin pans. In 1863, clever hydropathic health-food reformist, R.T. Trall, MD, wired together 12 rectangular pans exactly the size that he needed in order to bake his beloved graham gems, a staple of his fresh produce and whole grain based diet.

THE NEW GEM PAN

Trall's 1863 gem pan.
His recipe is on the facing page.

GEMS

"The bread described as "Gems" is by far the best bread that's at once wholesome, palatable, easy to masticate, and easily made. Stir together Graham flour and cold water to about the consistency of ordinary cup-cake batter. Bake in a hot oven in small tin patty pans, two inches square and three-fourths of an inch deep. If the pan's the right size, they'll rise one half, and be almost as light and porous as sponge cake." R.T. Trall

Ick. The only thing Trall's gems have going for them is fiber and the nutty flavor of freshly milled grains. Somebody liked them though, because you can find such recipes by the gem-pan-ful in vintage cookbooks. The thinking was that the "carbonic acid gas" in leavened products was somehow "injurious," so most recipes called for beating the flour and water mixture for 30 minutes in order to incorporate a little air into the rock-like cakes. Come the 1870s, home cooks who weren't freaked out by a little carbon dioxide gas began adding leavening, salt, milk, eggs, sugar and spices to the batter in order to get the gem muffins to taste better.

Around 1858, American foundries began to produce shallow cast iron egg and breakfast bread pans which later became "gem" irons, made in many, many shapes and sizes. I found mine at an antique shop for $50. You can get them for less, but this one was rust-free, seasoned and ready for baking. Notice the "gate marks" on the back of the pan. Prior to the 1870s, iron was poured in the middle of the underside of the pan leaving raised lines.

1859 Waterman Gem Pan

Later, the metal would be poured on the side of the pans and the edges filed down. Otherwise, the Lodge drop biscuit pan is just dandy for gems. I use it for cornbread, gems, English muffins and biscuits.

Back, Waterman Gem Pan

GEMS

There's just one itty bitty problem with my gem revolution. The mid-19th century gems are about as tasty as a dog chew toy. Just ask my dog, he loves them. The iron pans are terrific, as is the use of fresh ground whole grains, so I'm not giving up on them. On this page, I'm including some traditional graham gem recipes and then I'll move on to the doctored-up flavored gems.

"Gems are the simplest form of bread, using whole wheat or graham flour, salt and water, no leavening, no eggs."

A WATER-WHEEL MILL.

~Mrs. Lincoln's Boston Cook Book 1884

LIGHT AND HEALTHFUL GRAHAM GEMS
Dr. Chase's Third and Last Cook Book, 1887

"Sour milk, 2 cups; sugar, ½ cup; soda, ½ tea-spoonful; graham flour to stir thick; bake in iron gem pans, in a hot oven. Dr. Chase says, "Both light and healthful."

GRAHAM GEMS
North Adams Cook Book, 1905

Community cookbooks like this one compiled by women of the city of North Adams, MA are treasure troves of favorite hand-me-down family recipes. You gotta love the "walnut of butter" measurement in the first one. The second is actually a good whole wheat muffin (gem pans are really muffin-top pans!)

"Graham Gems.—One pint milk, one egg, three tablespoonfuls molasses, a walnut of butter, little salt, two teaspoonfuls Rumford's baking powder, graham flour to make stiff as cake. Bake in gem irons."

"Graham Gems.—One-third cup sugar, one cup sweet milk, one cup graham flour, one cup wheat flour, one egg, butter size of egg, two teaspoonfuls Rumford's baking powder. Bake in gem irons."

GEMS

AUNT BARB'S CRUNCHY CORNBREAD GEMS

Crunchy, buttery, exuberantly flavored cornbread that's as good at the fresh cornmeal you use to make them. Bake in gem pans, cornstick pans or a cast iron skillet. Great with butter and sorghum syrup (southern style molasses) or honey.

2 cups stone ground cornmeal	**1⅓ cups buttermilk**
1½ tsp. baking powder	**5 Tbs. melted butter**
¾ tsp. fine salt	**1 egg**

Preheat oven to 450°. Warm your gem pan in the hot oven for 10 minutes. In one bowl, mix dry ingredients; in another, whisk the wet. Add the wet to the dry and blend just until mixed. Drop a little piece of butter into each socket of the hot pan and fill ¾ full with batter. Bake about 15 minutes until brown on top. Serve with butter and sorghum syrup.

MRS. HILL'S POPOVERS
The Keene Cook Book, 1898

The *Keene Cook Book* by the Ladies First Congregational Church of Keene, New Hampshire, has oodles of gem recipes. Iron popover gem pans were deep, tapered, muffin pans.

"One pint of milk, two eggs, three even cups of flour, pinch of salt. Have the gem irons hot and well greased, and pour the mixture in. Bake fifteen minutes, with a hot fire. This makes fifteen cakes."

Author's note: Popovers are fantastic, but they're a bit challenging to master. Remember, "pop-unders" are just as good! Both new and antique iron popover (muffin) pans are widely available and they turn out a reliable popover. Whisk together the following room temperature ingredients:

1 cup milk, 1 cup AP flour, 1 Tbs. melted butter, 2 eggs, ½ tsp. fine salt
Preheat oven to 425°. Heat your cast iron popover pan, muffin pan (not nonstick) or custard cups a few minutes. Butter them and divide the batter between 11 cups. Bake 30 minutes without opening the oven. For the popover above, I added 1-inch chunks of cheddar cheese and a few fresh chives to the batter before baking. Always eat popovers hot out of the oven!

GEMS

MOM'S DIGESTIBLE FRUIT GEMS, 1906

American Motherhood Magazine's April 1906 edition contains heaps of unusual fruited gem recipes aimed at getting mothers to feed their youngsters healthy treats "free from the dangers accompanying the eating of indigestibles." But I thought you'd get a kick out of this granola gem recipe. Battle Creek's 1897 *Sanitarium Health Food Products Cook Book* describes granola as "a preparation of oats and wheat ready-cooked. It is excellent eaten with milk or cream, either hot or cold."

"GRANOLA GEMS. Into three-fourths of a cup of rich milk stir one cup of Granola. Drop into heated irons, and bake twenty minutes."

"APPLE GEMS. Chop fine 4 sour apples, add 1 beaten egg, 2 table-spoonfuls molasses, ½ cupfuls Indian corn meal, ½ cupfuls flour, ½ teaspoonful salt, 1 teaspoonful baking-powder. Add sufficient milk to make thick drop batter and bake in hot greased gem-pans."

Author's note: YUM! These apple cornmeal muffinettes really are good. Coarse-ground cornmeal adds a nice crunch to gems baked in iron pans. Here are just a couple adjustments to the above recipe:

> **"Indian corn meal" is an early word for cornmeal**
> **2 chopped apples instead of 4 (2 cups worth)**
> **2 Tbs. melted butter**
> **Milk, about 3 Tbs.**

Preheat your gem pan in a 425° oven a few minutes. Brush cups with butter. Divide batter and bake for about 15 minutes.

An optional crumble topping adds a bit of interest: Rub together **4 Tbs. butter with 2 packed Tbs. brown sugar and ½ cup AP flour.** Sprinkle the tops before baking. Resist the temptation to add cinnamon or other spices. Good cornmeal simply sings.

GEMS
Half-Cup Thirded Gems

Toss these brilliantly fragrant pebbled gems from their hot iron muffin pan onto a tea towel-lined basket in front of your guests and watch them squeal. No kidding, these are winners, and healthy too. In keeping with 19th century gem tradition, these thin muffins have very little sweetening so the flavors shine. They can be baked in any sort of muffin tin (not nonstick), but shallow muffins are best. Don't be put off by the lengthy list of ingredients. One of my cooking students takes a half-cup measure to the bulk food bins of her local market and easily collects just what she needs for a batch of these gems.

½ cup each of stoneground cornmeal, rye, whole wheat pastry (or regular whole wheat) and all-purpose flours
2 tsp. baking powder   1¼ cup buttermilk
¾ tsp. fine salt   2 Tbs. molasses
½ cup toasted pecans (opt.)   1 egg
Zest and juice of an orange   5 Tbs. unsalted butter
½ cup currants soaked in 3 Tbs. orange liqueur or juice.

Thirded gems in drop-biscuit pan

Whisk buttermilk, egg, molasses and melted butter together in one bowl. Combine dry ingredients together in another. Add wet to dry and stir in nuts and currants. Don't overmix! Drop into preheated buttered gem pans and bake in 425° oven until brown. One recipe makes two antique pans of gems or a dozen muffins.

Note: I keep a pint jar of Cointreau-soaked currants in the fridge at all times just in case I want to add them to my breads. Cover currants with the orange liqueur and refill with more fruit as needed.

LITTLE BREADS

Y ou definitely need a batter-splattered copy of social reformer, Lizzie Black Kander's *Settlement Cook Book*. Troubled by the late 19th century wave of Russian Orthodox Jewish immigrants living in horrible conditions in rundown Milwaukee neighborhoods, Lizzie Kander took action. She opened a "Settlement House" where immigrant women could come and learn English as well as homekeeping and cooking skills so that they could become more "Americanized" and less isolated in the rather primitive living conditions in which they found themselves. Kander sought to teach her ladies to cook their traditional Eastern European foods using American ingredients, while also throwing in some less "ethnic" dishes like this bread recipe below.

The wildly popular cookbook was a fundraiser for the community center and it's just full of wonderful German, Polish, Russian and American fare collected from a wide variety of women who contributed their best recipes to the project.

SETTLEMENT BREAD
Settlement Cook Book: The Way to a Man's Heart, 1915

2 cups scalded milk, or boiling water	*2 teaspoons fine salt*
1 tablespoon butter, or other fat	*1 tablespoon sugar*

½ oz. compressed yeast dissolved in ½ cup lukewarm water
6-6½ cups flour.

"Put salt, sugar and butter in large mixing bowl; pour on the hot milk or water; when lukewarm, add yeast and five cups flour, mix well with knife or mixing spoon. Add remaining flour, mix and turn the dough on a floured board and knead until soft and elastic. Put it back into the bowl, moisten, cover, and let it rise in a warm place until double its bulk, cut down, toss on floured board, then divide into loaves and place into greased or floured pans. Cover the bread and again allow it to double in bulk, then bake one hour in a hot oven, twelve seconds by the hand. Remove from pans and place in draft if you wish a hard crust. If a soft crust is desired, roll bread in a clean cloth. If set at night, use ½ cake yeast."

LITTLE BREADS

Lizzie Kander's enriched white Settlement bread recipe is a good foundation for rolls, cinnamon bread and monkey bread. An optional cup of whole wheat flour in the mix adds flavor. The buttermilk added to the recipe makes for tender, buttery rolls.

LIZZIE'S BUTTERMILK ROLLS

Evening Sponge (see page 19):
½ cup water, 1 scant cup AP flour (120g), pinch instant yeast
Dough:
Night before you bake, make your sponge. Next morning, combine your sponge, 2 cups buttermilk, 1 egg, 2 Tbs. softened butter. Stir in 2 tsp. fine salt, 1 Tbs. sugar, 1 tsp. instant yeast, 4½-5 cups AP flour (about 600 grams). Up to half of the flour can be whole wheat.

Follow Lizzie's *Settlement Bread* recipe mixing and rising instructions on the facing page. After the first rise, decide what you'd like to do with this roll recipe. You can make crescents, filled spirals, monkey bread or rolls of any shape. Let rise until doubled and bake in 400° oven about 20 minutes.

Herbed crescents: Divide dough into two balls. Roll each ball ¼-inch thick. Cut into pie-shaped wedges, brush with melted butter, sprinkle with chopped, fresh herbs, then roll up starting with the outside, large end.

Filled spirals: Roll half the dough into a rectangle. Sprinkle with grated cheese, roasted red peppers, cooked bacon, ham, or pancetta. Roll filled dough into a log, then slice into 1-inch thick slices. Let the slices rise, covered, on a parchment paper - lined cookie sheet until doubled. Preheat oven to 400 ° and bake about 20 minutes until browned.

Monkey bread: Chop dough into 1-inch pieces, roll in melted butter, then cinnamon sugar and place in a buttered vintage Pyrex refrigerator dish (or bread pan). Bake at 400° for 30 minutes until nicely browned. To eat, pull apart.

LITTLE BREADS

MRS. WELLES' GRIDDLE MUFFINS
Ten Dollars is Enough, Catherine Owen, 1889

Oh mercy me. Here's a fun cookbook about a spoiled young housewife, Molly, who has to manage her household on a mere ten bucks a week. We get a break from poor Molly's whining about how hard it is to teach her underpaid, young, inexperienced servant girl to cook when family friend, Mrs. Welles, comes to visit. Today, Mrs. Welles is going to teach us to make English muffins. *"Why they're as good two days old as one,"* says Molly. A gal with a tight budget has to learn to be happy with day-old bread, don't you know.

"It was Monday, and by the time the muffins had risen, washing would be over and the top of the fire free. "We'll go out and set them now," says Mrs. Welles. The setting was very simple, being only the making of a stiff bread-sponge. Half a cake of yeast was dissolved in a pint and a half of warm milk, into which a scant tea-spoonful of salt, two of sugar and one large one of butter warmed, were stirred. Into this as much dry, sifted flour was mixed (about three pints) as would make an exceedingly stiff batter, in fact "stiffer than batter, softer than dough " may serve as an indication of the consistency, or "almost too stiff to stir, quite too soft to knead." When this was beaten long and hard, one third was put into another bowl and this was thinned down with warm milk to a batter that would pour slowly. This was for crumpets, the only difference between the two being in consistency. They were covered and put behind the range to rise."

While the dough rises, the ladies take a break to prepare beef hearts and soused mackerel. Lucky for you, I will spare you the details. They cook the muffins by dropping a spoonful of batter the size of a "duck egg" on a soapstone griddle. The perfectly browned muffins are fork-split, toasted, buttered and served, just in time for tea.

LITTLE BREADS

MOLLY'S WHOLE WHEAT ENGLISH MUFFINS

Molly is right about one thing, English muffins do keep well for a couple days on the counter, and they freeze beautifully. You can drop the batter onto an iron skillet, but you'll have taller, prettier muffins if you use muffin rings, available at kitchen stores. The Lodge drop biscuit pan works even better. Here's how to make half of Mrs. Welles' muffin recipe fresh in the morning for breakfast. The recipe makes 10 muffins. Start your sponge 24 hours before you bake.

Morning Sponge (see page 19):
　½ cup water, 1 scant cup (120g) AP flour, pinch instant yeast
Evening dough::

1¼ cup warm milk	1 cup (130g) whole wheat flour
1 Tbs. honey	1¼ cup (162g) AP flour
1 Tbs. softened butter	1½ tsp. fine salt
¾ tsp. instant yeast	

In the morning, mix your sponge. That evening, (the night before you bake), make the dough. Combine the sponge, milk, honey and butter and stir well. Then add the dry ingredients and beat the batter with a spoon for a few minutes. Cover and refrigerate overnight. In the morning, warm the bowl over hot water for just a minute. In about an hour, the dough should be puffy and ready to bake. Heat your skillet to medium-low on your stovetop and grease the inside of the muffin rings. Throw a little cornmeal down on the griddle and inside

Cookstove English muffins in drop biscuit pan.

the rings. Use a ¼-cup measure to gently scoop out enough dough to almost fill the rings. Let the muffins cook on medium-low till they're lightly browned on the bottom. Flip the muffin, ring and all, and continue to bake, about 15 minutes total. To serve, fork split, toast and then butter. Orange marmalade's awfully good on a crispy hot English muffin!

BIALYS

I am counting on you NOT knowing what a Bialy is. Because if you are a bialy-eater, then the only ones you like are the ones you're used to eating. In that spirit, I give you my Dad's version of Bialys, and he knows a thing or two about these chewy, oniony, tradition-steeped rolls.

Lesser known as bialystokers, these round flattened rolls were brought to New York City in the early 1900s by Jewish immigrants from Bialystoker, Poland. My dad's parents, also Polish and Russian Jews, likewise landed in NYC, fleeing persecution following the 1917 Bolshevik revolution. It's a sad story, indeed, the eventual fate of the Jews of the city of Bialystoker and its nearby neighboring eastern European countries during the reign of Hitler's Nazi Germany. All the more reason for the passion evoked by the simple act of eating these delicious rolls.

To this day, my dad, Leon Swell, longs for the bialys, bagels, and the giant, dark, robustly flavored pumpernickel rye breads of his depression-era New York City childhood. He fondly remembers picking up the family bread from steamy, hot underground ovens manned by older Russian Jewish immigrant men with big, burly arms. When Leon isn't working in his dramatically beautiful, large native garden in Richmond, VA, you can find him in his kitchen grinding the grains for today's bake. Pumpernickel rye, pletzel and bialystokers are among his favorite breads.

Photo courtesy of the Library of Congress

BIALYS

On a recent visit with my dad, we made a bialy documentary to pass on to family members and to you! They are traditionally made with lots of yeast, very high gluten bread flour and plenty of salt. Watch out, these guys smell better than anything on this earth while they're baking! Bialys are best eaten straight out of the oven as they stale rapidly, which is a pity. Or not, if you don't mind stuffing yourself silly when the moment is right.

Real bialy bakers, my dad included, do not retard the dough overnight in the fridge as I do. To be more authentic, increase the yeast in this recipe to a tablespoon and each rising of the dough will take under an hour. The overnight chill adds flavor, texture and longevity. I'm starting my own tradition!

An hour before you bake, place a baking stone (if you have one) in the oven to heat at 475°. This will be about the time you divide the dough into individual rounds and prepare the filling.

ONION POPPYSEED BIALYSTOKERS

2½ cups (325g) bread flour (bread flour is a must!)
1 heaping tsp. fine salt   **1 cup ice water**
½ tsp. instant yeast   **1 tsp. honey (opt.)**

Mix all until just combined and then let it sit 30 minutes. Knead in mixer 7 minutes on speed 2 or at least 20 minutes by hand, then cover and refrigerate overnight. Next day, bring dough up to room temperature, about 2 hours. Divide dough into 10 pieces and form into balls, seam side down.

Continued on page 60 ...

BIALYS

Continued from page 59 ...

Roll each ball in rye flour, if you have it (fresh ground, says Leon, for old-time flavor) and let rest, covered, 45 minutes on a cornmeal-dusted baking sheet. Now, use a spice jar or small glass and smush pockets in the dough to hold the onion and poppyseed filling. At this point you can decide if you want a fat puffy bialy or a chewy thin one. I like them well-smushed in the middle so that the thin layer of dough under the innards gets crispy from the hot baking stone.

ONION POPPYSEED FILLING

Chop a medium yellow onion into small pieces and add up to a tablespoonful of poppyseeds, a pinch of salt and a glug of vegetable oil ... about a tablespoon.

Fill the bialys with a spoonful of this raw mixture as is, or you can caramelize the onions for 15 minutes in the oil first, then stir in the seeds and proceed to filling the bialy holes. Try both ways and see what you prefer.

After filling the rolls, slide the baking sheet into the hot oven. If you're using a baking stone, you can nudge the bialys directly onto the stone after they've baked a few minutes. Bake for about 15 minutes, depending on size, until they're nice and brown.

Leon Swell, bialy baker!

WAR BREAD

World-wide food shortages brought on by the ravages of World War I, prompted Herbert Hoover's 1917 Food Administration to insist that all Americans consume and waste less refined wheat, fat, sugar, meat and eggs. At a time when 60% of American housewives baked their own breads, don't you know that they felt the pinch when asked to substitute all or part of the flour in their beloved white bread with whole grains.

But step up to the plate, they did. The resulting make-do recipes from this era are inspiring. Breads made from grains such as barley, oats, rye, buckwheat, rice, whole wheat and corn were creative, wholesome and often gluten-free. Americans maintained the palate and understanding of the need for whole-grained breads in their diets clear through the 1940s until, again, back crept the soft, spongy, flavorless, white breads ... a sure sign of prosperity!

Save a loaf
a week
help win
the war

RESTRICTED
Walt Mason, *Farm Journal Magazine*, 1918

I do not like the sawdust bread I eat three times a day;
I'd like a nice white loaf instead—but nothing do I say.
Our fighting soldiers need the wheat, to keep their strength and heft,
and I am thankful I may eat whatever stuff is left.
So bring along your wooden loaf, and slice it with a saw;
I am no cheap, disloyal oaf, the line at that to draw.
I like some sugar in my tea, I like it on my rice,
but Hoover lately said to me, "Make one more sacrifice!
If sugar from your board you shoo, you may some Teuton halt."
And so I make the fragrant brew, and sweeten it with salt.
I'm eating things that I detest, I'm drinking things I hate,
and all the time I do my best to keep my smile on straight.
With cheerful brow, with queenly grace, obey all rules in sight;
the patriot with grouchy face is only half-way right.

WAR BREAD

Oat-meal Bread.   Helen McHorly

Pour 2½ cups of boiling water over 1 cup rolled oats, add 1 tablespoon sugar, 1 tablespoon salt, 1 tablespoon shortening not-melted, let cook, when luke warm add 1 yeast-cake dissolved in a little warm water, stir in flour enough to make a stiff dough, knead, let rise over night, form in loaves, let rise and bake in rather a slow oven about one hour.

HELEN'S OATMEAL BREAD, 1918

My nineteen-teens handwritten recipe book has lots of war-time recipes for oatmeal bread. Here's one that's a bit difficult to read, but I wanted you to see the lovely handwriting. Below is a very moist, fantastic, grainier version of Helen's oatmeal bread. It's great for sandwiches when baked in a loaf pan that's been buttered and sprinkled with oats. Your whole family will love this bread!

Evening sponge (see page 19):
      1 scant cup (120g) AP flour, ½ cup water, pinch yeast.
Dough:

1½ cups old fashioned oats	2½ cups water
2¾ tsp. fine salt	1 Tbs. softened butter
2 cups (260g) whole wheat flour	2 Tbs. honey
1 cup (130g) bread flour	1 tsp. instant yeast
1 cup (130g) bread flour (reserved)	

The night before you bake:
Make your sponge and set aside.
Cook together the oats, 2½ cups water, and salt just a few minutes until thickened. Cover and refrigerate.

Continued ...

WAR BREAD

Oatmeal Bread, continued ...

Next morning:
Into a bowl, stir your sponge and your oats until well mixed. Add the honey and softened butter. Combine 1 tsp. yeast with two cups (260g) whole wheat flour and mix into your wet ingredients. Let the mixture sit about 15 minutes to absorb the moisture. Now add another cup (130g) bread flour and start to knead.

As you knead, the dough will become stickier as the oats release their moisture, so you'll need at least ½ cup of the additional bread flour. After about 10 min-

FOOD WILL WIN THE WAR
You came here seeking Freedom
You must now help to preserve it

WHEAT is needed for the allies
Waste nothing

utes, you'll have a smooth dough that's still soft. Place in a buttered bowl and let it rise, covered, about 2 hours until doubled. Divide the dough in half and form into 2 loaves. Place in bread pans that have been buttered and sprinkled with oats. Let rise another 1½ hours, slash a couple times, and then bake in a 400° oven for 15 minutes. Turn heat to 375° and bake until done (200° internal temp.), about 20 more minutes. You can also form into round loaves, brush the tops with egg white and sprinkle with oats before baking. If baking in a preheated covered pan, remove the lid after 15 minutes and continue to bake as above.

WAR BREAD

2 cups boiling water	2 tablespoons fat
2 tablespoons sugar	6 cups rye flour
1½ teaspoons salt	1½ cups whole wheat flour
¼ cup lukewarm water	1 cake yeast

To the boiling water, add the sugar, fat and salt. When lukewarm, add the yeast which has been dissolved in the lukewarm water. Add the rye and whole wheat flour. Cover and let rise until twice its bulk, shape into loaves; let rise until double and bake about 40 minutes in a moderately hot oven,

WAR BREAD

POTATO PARKER HOUSE ROLLS
Foods That Will Win the War, 1918

Unfurl your red-checked tablecloth and pass around a basket of these homey, voluptuous rolls. You'll need about five per person! These light, flaky, wheat-conserving savory breadlets delight in the addition of chopped fresh herbs and parmesan, or other firm tangy cheese. Form into rolls, burger buns, or a loaf. This recipe makes about two dozen rolls or two small loaves.

½ cake yeast	*3½ cups flour*
1 cup milk	*2 cups potato (mashed and warm)*
1 teaspoon fat	*1 teaspoon salt*
1 egg	*3 tablespoons corn syrup*

"Dissolve yeast in lukewarm milk. Stir in dry ingredients. Add potato and knead until smooth. Let rise until light. Roll thin, fold over, bake until brown."

UPDATED VERSION

Evening sponge (see page 19):
   ¼ cup water, ½ cup AP flour, pinch yeast.

Dough:

2 Tbs. honey	2 cups warm mashed potato (2 large baking potatoes)
¾ cup milk	3½ cups (455g) AP flour (1 cup can be whole wheat)
2 Tbs. butter	1¾ tsp. fine salt
1 egg	1 tsp. instant yeast

Boil peeled potatoes, drain, mash roughly and cool until just warm. Mix potato and sponge with wet ingredients, then add dry and knead about 5-10 minutes. It's a soft dough, so add as little extra flour as possible in order to be able to knead lightly. Let rise in buttered bowl until doubled, about 90 minutes. Roll lightly about ½-inch for rolls, and cut with a 2 or 3-inch cutter (a muffin ring is perfect), butter tops, then fold over. You can sprinkle a few fresh herbs and a grating of parmesan on each roll before folding. Place on a parchment-lined or buttered cookie sheet, cover with a clean towel and let rise another hour. Slide parchment onto heated baking stone if you have one, and bake at 375° until nicely browned, about 10-15 minutes.

MARMALADE

ORANGE MARMALADE

You're going to need a simple orange marmalade recipe to go with all the whole grain breads in this book ... if you are the marmalade type, that is. Feel free to mix orange varieties; any thin-skinned oranges or tangerines will do. This recipe makes a beautiful clear, tart orange jelly with lots of pieces of tender rind. It's not as bitter as some versions. Great on toast, in your apple pie and even in your tea!

1½ lb. mixed thin skinned organic oranges
Juice of 2 lemons   3½ cups sugar (approx.)
6 cups water   Cheesecloth

Cut the oranges in half and juice. Juice lemons. Remove pulp and seeds of oranges and tie up in a piece of cheesecloth. Thinly slice the orange peels and halve. Boil juices, orange peel and water 10 minutes, refrigerate overnight. Next day, simmer orange mixture along with the bag of seeds and pulp (your pectin) for about 45 minutes covered. Uncover pan and simmer until liquid is reduced by half and the peel is really tender. Add the sugar and cook until mixture reaches 220°. If you don't have a thermometer, check the set by drizzling a small amount of jam on a saucer that's been placed in the freezer. If it stays put when you drag your finger through the jam, then it's ready. It will look runny but it will thicken up. Fill 4 sterilized half pint canning jars, screw on fresh lids and place in boiling water bath for about 10 minutes. You can also just refrigerate the jam in jars, unprocessed. It will keep a month or two.

Straw-berry Bread. Take of the berries, Bray them in a Mortar, mix them with meal, and make them into Strawberry Bread.

Early American Cookery, 1896

RESOURCES

RECOMMENDED POTS FOR BAKING HISTORIC BREADS

BREAD PANS

For these historic breads, it's best to use a pan that is taller than it is wide. I prefer glass. Vintage colored pyrex is charming, but clear is better for viewing. Anchor Hocking makes an especially good tall, narrow 1.12-quart bread glassware pan that comes with a plastic cover for storage. Available at kitchen stores.

CAST IRON PANS

Lodge (American-made)   *www.lodgemfg.com*
Drop Biscuit pan is a gem pan.
Combo Cooker is a skillet with a flat lid.
Dutch Ovens Get one with iron lid, not glass; I prefer 5-quart.
Camp Dutch Ovens with feet and recessed lids are meant for live-fire baking. You can also bake with them in your oven. The 4-quart (10-inch) is good for these breads, but the 6-quart, (12-inch) is my favorite because you can put a 9-inch pie plate on top of a couple metal canning jar rings and bake pies, biscuits, cakes, etc.
Le Creuset (French-made*)*   *http://cookware.lecreuset.com*
Ooh-la-la. Beautiful enameled cast iron pots, you can bake bread in the round or oval French ovens that come in a plethora of sizes and colors. 4½ or 5½-quart for these breads, but you can make do with any size. Remove the handle and stuff hole with foil.

CERAMIC BAKEWARE

Emil Henry ovenware   *www.emilehenryusa.com*
Beautiful French-made high-temperature ceramic ovenware in many sizes. For these breads, 5.5-quart or 4.2-quart.
Sassafrass La Cloche is a large, domed stoneware pot (pictured on page 29) that makes great bread. I love it. Available online at many sources, but I like Breadtopia.   *www.breadtopia.com*
They also sell everything you can think of for making bread, from baking stones for your oven to wonderful proofing basket liners.
Baking Stones. Get the largest you can find for your oven. 16x4-inch is best. Granite is also super for baking on, though it needs to live in your oven. Baking stones available many places, including Breadtopia and King Arthur Flour   *www.kingarthurflour.com*

RESOURCES

OTHER USEFUL BREAD BAKING GIZMOS

Campfire Dutch oven lid lifter, available at Lodge (see left)
Digital thermometer, side display, under 10-second read. Widely available, try Breadtopia or King Arthur (see left). $15-$25 is fine.
Digital Scale ... You need a scale. I like *Escali*, the least expensive one will do, about $25. Available at kitchen stores or King Arthur Flour.
Grain Mills for home use. Get a good one. Pleasant Hill Grain *www.pleasanthillgrain.com* has a great selection. I have a Country Living Manual Mill, KoMo electric is a good one as is Nutrimill.

A SMATTERING OF HELPFUL WEBSITES

Aunt Barb's blog   *www.logcabincooking.blogspot.com*
Fresh Loaf forum   *www.thefreshloaf.com*
John C. Campbell Folk School (classes)   *www.folkschool.org*
Bread Bakers Guild of America   *http://www.bbga.org*

SOURCING REGIONAL FLOURS AND GRAINS

Easier said than done! You'll have to root around to find locally grown and milled flours in your part of the country. Your town grocery, co-op, organic markets and farmer's markets are a good place to start. Also ask your favorite artisan bakers where they purchase their flours. I find it helpful to follow links in websites devoted to organic grain growing and artisan baking such as:

NC Organic Bread Flour Project   *http://ncobfp.blogspot.com*
Heritage Wheat Conservancy   *www.growseed.org/seed*
The Kneading Conference ... lots of information and leads
http://kneadingconference.com   *http://kneadingconferencewest.com*

SPOOM, Society for the Preservation of Old Mills *www.spoom.org*
You'll love the interactive map where you can locate the historic mills in your state. You will certainly find cornmeal at these sites.

A FEW MAIL ORDER FLOUR & GRAIN SITES

Anson Mills, Charleston, SC   *www.ansonmills.com*
Heartland Mill, Marienthal, KS   *www.heartlandmill.com*
West Wind Milling Co., Linden, MI   *http://westwindmilling.com*

RECOMMENDED READING

The following books are current, well-tested, instructive books on how to make a variety of breads with tons of information and illustrations. There are many, many good bread books available now, thanks to the ever-growing international interest in artisan breads. Each book (except for the last two science books) is penned by a professional baker with his or her own approach to creating their breads, ranging from easy to methodical.

Artisan Breads Every Day, **Peter Reinhart, 2009**
The Bread-baker's Apprentice, **Peter Reinhart, 2001**
> Peter Reinhart is an excellent instructor, and all of his books are user-friendly, even for the novice baker. He's endlessly fascinated by bread, and I guarantee his enthusiasm will rub off on you.

Bread, A Book of Techniques & Recipes, **Jeffrey Hamelman, 2004**
> Way informative, includes formulas for home bakers and professionals, alike. Perfect for a bread-obsessed home baker.

Bread Matters, **Andrew Whitley, 2006**
> For home cooks, written by passionate British baker & instructor

English Bread and Yeast Cookery, **Elizabeth David, 1977**
> The "it" book of historic bread. You must invite Elizabeth David's thorough, timeless and delightful book into your life! Five busy years in the making, this is a comprehensive and approachable work by one of the best food writers of our time.

My Bread, **Jim Lahey 2009**
> Lahey popularized the no-knead artisan bread method when Mark Bittman wrote an article for the New York Times about Lahey's "Anybody-can-make-great -artisan-bread" recipe in 2006. EASY to make breads (without pre-ferments), baked in cast iron pots.

Tartine Bakery, **Chad Robertson, 2010**
> Artisan, sourdough breads baked in cast iron pots.

The Bread Builders, **Daniel Wing and Alan Scott, 1999**
> Sourdough breads and plans for building a wood-fired bread oven

On Food and Cooking, Science & Lore of the Kitchen, **Harold McGee, 2004**
> Anything you ever wanted to know about food and science (which is what bread is), is here in this big, reader-friendly tome.

Bread Science, **Emily Buehler, 2009** Order from *www.twobluebooks.com*

BIBLIOGRAPHY

A Treatise on Bread, Sylvester Graham, 1837
The English Bread Book, Eliza Acton, 1857
Appledore Cook Book, Maria Parloa, 1872
Aunt Mary's New England Cook Book, 1881
Bread and the Principles of Bread Making, Helen Atwater, 1900
Camp Cooking, Frank Bates, 1915
Hydropathic Cook Book, RT Trall, 1863
Complete Bread Baker, J Thompson Gill 1881
Cook Book, Debbie Coleman, 1855
Dr. Chase's Third and Last Cook Book, AL Chase, 1887
Foods That Will Win the War, Goudiss and Goudiss, 1917
Good Cookery Illustrated, Augusa Llanover,1867
Household Recipes, Lilly Haxworth Wallace, 1902
Mrs. Lincoln's Boston Cook Book 1884; also revised edition, 1896
North Adams Cook Book, 1905
Practical Breadmaking, Frederick Vine, 1897
The Camper's Handbook, Thomas Holdling, 1908
The History of Bread, John Ashton, London, 1902
The *Keene Cook Book,* Ladies First Congregational Church, 1898
The Virginia Housewife, Mary Randolph, *1833*
The Young Millwright and Miller's Guide, Oliver Evans, 1848
Uncle Sam's Advice to Housewives, 1917
The New System of Making Bread, Robert Wells, 1903

American Farm and Home Magazine, 1889
American Kitchen Magazine, 1900
American Motherhood Magazine April 1906
Arthur's Home Magazine, 1869
Cultivator and Country Gentleman, 1866
Farm Journal Magazine, 1918
Good Housekeeping, August, 1886, September, 1889
Michigan Farmer Magazine, 1888
New England Kitchen Magazine, 1895
The Century Illustrated Magazine, December, 1883
The Housekeeper, August, 1880
USDA Farmer's Bulletin, 1894

CARING FOR CAST IRON

You've returned from antiquing with your lovely vintage, rusted antique gem pan in hand. What now?

To remove rust: Try steel wool first or a bit of sandpaper. For more serious rust, use a drill with a wire brush attachment.

To remove baked-on gunk: Some people spray with oven cleaner and place in a zip-lock bag for a couple days, and then carefully wash (with gloves). Others use a wire brush as above.

Seasoning: Wipe the pan lightly with solid fat or oil. I prefer solid coconut oil; others use lard, Crisco, vegetable oil. I find that oil leaves a sticky finish. Place in 400° oven upside-down over a cookie sheet and let it bake for an hour, then leave in oven another hour with heat off. Repeat if pan is new and unseasoned or if it's been sanded.

Everyday cleaning and seasoning: To maintain the nonstick cooking surface, wash with warm water and, if needed, a very mild soap like Dr. Bronner's. I season my iron Dutch oven, gem and muffin pans every time I use them by rubbing lightly with a bit of coconut oil while they're still warm from washing. Use a paper towel to soak up excess oil.

Thanks ... to Steve Millard, Toe River Design, for front and back cover design. Proofreaders were Janet Swell, Carolyn Dickson, and Jennifer Thomas. The ever-persistent recipe testers included Wyndy Bonesteel, Richard Renfro, Mark Rosenstein, Janet Swell, Jennifer Thomas (Montford Walk-in Bakery), Courtney Webb, & Laura Wright. Thanks to the throngs of taste-testers. Office staff, Kelli Churchill, John Miller, and Wayne Erbsen win the carb award. Runners-up tasters were my kids, Rita and Wes Erbsen, Annie & Gianluca DeBacco, friends Jennifer, Cece & Neil Thomas, Natalya Weinstein, Renate Rikkers and Paul, Wyndy, Jonah, and Luke Bonesteel. Thanks to Dave Bauer of Farm & Sparrow bakery in Asheville for his fantastic home-grown and milled grains for recipe testing. Appreciation to Dudley Wilson for popping in to drop off ancient tattered recipe books he runs across. And to my Dad, Leon Swell, thanks for support and inspiration. Finally, thanks to my husband and publisher, Wayne Erbsen, for not squashing my silliness and for eating way too much bread this year!

RECIPE INDEX

NATIVE GROUND MUSIC

MORE HISTORIC COOKBOOKS BY BARBARA SWELL

A Garden Supper Tonight
The First American Cookie Lady
The Lost Art of Pie Making Made Easy
Old-Time Farmhouse Cooking
Secrets of the Great Old-Timey Cooks
Mama's in the Kitchen
Children at the Hearth
Take Two and Butter 'Em While They're Hot!
Log Cabin Cooking

BOOKS OF SONGS , LORE & COOKING

Backpocket Bluegrass Songbook
Backpocket Old-Time Songbook
Cowboy Songs, Jokes & Lingo
Front Porch Songs & Stories
Log Cabin Pioneers
Early American Cookery

Bluegrass Gospel Songbook
Outlaw Ballads & Lore
Railroad Fever
Songs of the Civil War
Rural Roots of Bluegrass
Pioneer Village Cookbook

MUSIC INSTRUCTION BOOKS

Bluegrass Banjo for the Complete Ignoramus
Clawhammer Banjo for the Complete Ignoramus
Bluegrass Mandolin for the Complete Ignoramus
Flatpicking Guitar for the Complete Ignoramus
Old-Time Fiddle for the Complete Ignoramus
Bluegrass Jamming on Banjo
Bluegrass Jamming on Fiddle
Bluegrass Jamming on Mandolin
Southern Mountain Instruction Books:
Banjo, Fiddle, Guitar, Mandolin, and Dulcimer

FOR A FREE CATALOG, CONTACT US AT:

Native Ground Books & Music
109 Bell Road, Asheville, NC 28805
(800) 752-2656
www.nativeground.com   banjo@nativeground.com
www.logcabincooking.blogspot.com